Instagram Marketing 2019

Secrets and Hacks Top Influencers Use to Grow and Monetize Their Personal Brand and Business

Written By Mark Hollister

The reproduction, transmission, and duplication of any of the content found herein, including any specific or extended information will be done as an illegal act regardless of the end form the information ultimately takes. This includes copied versions of the work both physical, digital and audio unless express consent of the Publisher is provided beforehand. Any additional rights reserved.

Furthermore, the information that can be found within the pages described forthwith shall be considered both accurate and truthful when it comes to the recounting of facts. As such, any use, correct or incorrect, of the provided information will render the Publisher free of responsibility as to the actions taken outside of their direct purview. Regardless, there are zero scenarios where the original author or the Publisher can be deemed liable in any fashion for any damages or hardships that may result from any of the information discussed herein.

Additionally, the information in the following pages is intended only for informational purposes and should thus be thought of as universal. As befitting its nature, it is presented without assurance regarding its prolonged validity or interim quality. Trademarks that are mentioned are done without written consent and can in no way be considered an endorsement from the trademark holder.

Table of contents

Introduction

The invention and rapid growth of technology have affected a lot of things, even marketing. Everything has become easy with technology. The stress of doing things such as marketing has been curtailed. You don't need to get a huge amount of money to do your marketing. This age says "market your product with your technology, your smartphones." Every brand and business builder has, since 2015, leveraged on using technology to market and grow their business. The technology used in this context refers to social media platforms such as Instagram and Facebook. However, our scope of studies here is on Instagram. We want to unravel the hidden treasures therein because most writings have been on Facebook. Even though you might have been on this platform for quite some times now, you barely know these tricks and secrets. Little worries, you are on your way to learning this same thing, as top influencers have used them in simple, precise and practical ways using Instagram. This book is based on marketing hacks and tricks used to grow and even monetize an account, compiled from top influencers of users of Instagram. You are learning how to use that your smartphone es to promote your brand and business. To harness Instagram and personal branding in the growth of the business, this book has been strategically designed as if it were in two parts appendix with a bonus –to expose the secrets and hacks of Instagram and personal branding.

At the beginning of this book, you will learn Instagram as marketing vendor, its benefits, why you will need to advertise on it, how to increase the fan base, how to grow 20,000 followers with practical steps, and how to convert your followers to clients. In fact, every trick used on Instagram will be practically dealt with. You will have to be with your phone and have your data connection intact in order to get the fullness of this book.

The latter part of this book is devoted to personal branding as another means of grow your business and brand. The aim is to cross-analyze personal branding and Instagram branding. You will learn the benefits of branding personally, how to incorporate a unique selling proposition into your personal branding, how to access opportunities that can take your brand to the next level, and how to use business storytelling to sell products in both physical and online marketplaces. Personal branding is actually cool and fine, but Instagram marketing is exceptional.

There is a bonus in this book. This could be regarded as the third part, and it is based on using Instagram automated tools. These are machines basically hone to providing, without effort, automation for your Instagram. You will learn these tools, how to use them and their examples.

It is pertinent to note that every step is given, though from top influencers, are not alpha and omega. They are not applied in a wishy-washy manner. It is subject to lots of circumstances that are natural, thus, uncontrollable. Study with all doggedness the kind of business you are doing and define how you will grow it. The steps here are practical prototypes for you. Grow through them with all alacrity; apply them when necessary; key into the flow.

The Instagram platform is unique because a wide range of people can be covered with just simple steps. The development of Instagram has been redirected to suit marketing. You will wonder how logging into your account and uploading of pictures could grow your brand and even monetize it. The Instagram operation is based on visuals. By visual, it includes graphics, videos, and photos. With this operation, you can grow your business. How foolish is this? Stay tuned and follow this book step-by-step. Don't forget that having your phone (either Android or iPhone) with a good internet connection to follow the steps is the key. There are lots of things engraved in this gem. You will be glad you gave it a trial. The world is at your tip. You will carry out marketing in your comfort zone. Less talk, get to work!

Chapter 1: Instagram as Marketing Vendor

Every business owner wants their business to grow –and such is you. The growth of a business, generally, is championed on 'how aware people are' of the product. In the same vein, Marketing is the process of promoting, growing and selling a product –the backbone of a business. The aim of branding one's product made much business minded people to seek a fast-growing platform such as Instagram. Likewise, the growth of smartphones and iPhones (on which Instagram app has been designed) within the fall of 2011 to date is alarming. The world, at large, has adopted the smart mobile world; the usage of smartphones for business promotion. The adoption of this app has created a revolution in the experiences people have online especially on social media like Instagram. In the examination of the uniqueness of Instagram as a marketing vendor, Klinker explained that "Instagram has in recent years emerged as the most successful platform for photos." This is because the origin of this fast-growing platform could be traced to ordinary uploading of photos. How could this have been converted into a marketing platform is part of the aims of this book? In Klinker's words "what initially began as a small platform for a few thousand people who shared interesting content about their lives, evolved over time into a platform with more than 300 million users (April 2015). The message is clear: 300 million users is a huge amount of people to hit with your brand and business promotion. The recent report on the number of people using Instagram increased with 100 million compared to the recent report that gave a total of 400 million users. This means that you will promote your brand simply by uploading pictures and not only that, monetize the picture uploaded. Interesting right? Good!

One of the factors that contributed to the usage of Instagram as a marketing vendor is the easy accessibility of the app and its mode of operation. The advent of technology can't be denied. Instagram is one of the most influencing social media platforms that operate mainly with media uploads. Many people have been aware of the platform but very few people market or monetize their account. The purpose of this book is to guide you through the processes, with practical examples of growing your own account and brand. The solution to promoting your brand by marketing it through a medium of over 300million users. Of course, everyone will not like your post, this is not because your pictures are bad but because you have not unleashed the secrets et and hacks top influencers have been using to promote themselves. It is very simple, download the app, create an account and get started.

It is pertinent to note that the guides given in this book are not operating by hook and lines; rather their effectiveness is based on many natural issues. You will surely learn the secrets and hacks which I believe you will apply while learning them. The secret of the success Instagram has experienced sequel basically to its easy use as an app and the content of it. The huge and increasing number of users have made many business developers find it an interesting platform to engage lots of audience within a short and fast scale. The audience though passive, yet with great impact, are involved in the awareness of the product.

According to a report on how people have migrated from the traditional way of marketing their product to the usage of smartphones, sited by McGraw-Hill, on September 9, 2012, CNNMoney.com reported that Apple's revenue from iPhone sales alone (at $74.3 billion within 12 months) exceeded all Microsoft's product lines combined (at 73 billion within 12 months too). What effect does this have? It shows that many prefer to use the smartphone more than the word. Instagram has leveraged on this opportunity which will enable you to become a prolific Instagram marketer with few steps. There are secrets to how top influencers have used this judiciously to achieve their goals and even monetize their account. Follow this book as you will be led, step by step, to the hacks and secrets!

Chapter 2: Why Advertising on Instagram?

Having been introduced to Instagram as a marketing vendor, let us examine what advertisement is and the reason for choosing to advertise on Instagram above other social media platforms. An advertisement is a public solicitation strategically crafted to aid the selling of a commodity or any similar services. Instagram is a multi-million users platform where over 1 million people could be online at the same time. The first thing to consider before migrating to a smartphone is to be ready to use it wholeheartedly as it has proven over the years to be an effective platform. To get an insight on the number of traffics generated on smartphone and how fast they are, McGraw-Hill gave a report through questions and answers: Does Internet traffic from mobile devices exceed that of desktop web surfers in any large number? He answered this by saying in India. Mobile Internet surpassed desktop traffic in May 2012 (Meeker). He continued to say that the trend is occurring in other countries as well and will continue to become the new style. Which is faster; the 4G LTE mobile network or high-speed DSL for your home? He answered this, reporting that according to digitaltrends.com, in head-to-head comparisons of which internet services were the fastest, the Verizon 4G LTE network performed better than high-speed DSL. It was not as good as the top tier. Many users on Instagram has been one of the reasons Instagram is used as a marketing platform. This means that posting pictures alongside using some special features already made available on the app will skyrocket your advertisement; wide promotion of your brand.

The popular Ben and Jerry's Ice cream, a smart Instagram marketer, is a top leading team that uses the platform for advertisement. This is because of the rapid growth of Instagram users according to Hill, increased from 887,000 daily active users to 7.3 million (comScore). Many of the teams have piggybacked on this fast-growing internet server to reach the large and varying audience. In the report of Hill on Ben and Jerry's ice cream team on how they engaged their audience, asking the fans to "capture euphoria" and share it on Instagram by taking a picture with your Ben and Jerry's ice cream, upload it on Instagram, and include the hashtag #captureeuphoria. This is a simple process that will be explained in the course of this book –little worries. Tracing the inception of mobile marketing, we will know that the path was becoming clearer to what we have today which will still be more. Many people, however, have tried to use many platforms such as Facebook for marketing their commodities. This did not proof landmark success upon the invention of Instagram, based on reports. Amazingly, Instagram was exclusively built for the social network on mobile devices. It is the founder of it all. It was discovered that the strategies used are now more effective with Instagram. More importantly, Instagram was born to be mobile friendly. Little wonder, it was developed specifically for iPhones and subsequently adapted to Android. The special features such as the one given (hashtag) are one of the basic reasons Instagram is the best choice for smart marketers like you. The ability to post pictures to a wide range of people within a considerable short time space makes Instagram the best of all. While other platforms have the same feature (posting pictures), Instagram aims at giving keen features to the pictures which ensure 'liking,' following and promoting the account that posted the pictures. The features contained on Instagram as well as aim at popularizing the users' account.

The app is very easy to reach, and the interface is user-friendly. Everyone can easily operate the app as it is not built with much difficulty like other social media platforms. Meanwhile, Instagram was mainly used from inception for uploading pictures while people like and follow one another. It is used from 2015 till now beyond these features. The developers have changed the look and added many features too to suit the goal of Instagram.

In conclusion, Instagram is best for brand and business advertisement because it has a number of users whose increment is very promising. You can reach a good number of people from across the whole world by just uploading product pictures only. Don't forget that products can barely be explained without their visual appearance to enhance it —this is the strength of Instagram advertisement. The process is very simple: upload your product pictures, people will like it, hit your contact and you get potential buyers! Instagram Advertisement, simple and effective product promotion.

Chapter 3: What are the benefits of creating a Business Account?

To create an account on Instagram is not enough and effective. You have to, in order to enjoy Instagram marketing opportunities, create or convert your account to a business one. In the latter part of this book, you will learn the steps to creating a business account. In this section, however, you will learn some key benefits of having a business account. Everyone clamors on how important Instagram has been or will be to one's business, but you wonder how on earth this is important. Stay calm and follow this section on the benefits of creating a business account. The deal is creating a business account from a personal account. Business accounts have special features. The tasks of creating an account with such features given above are worth doing for the following reasons given, according to Claire Brenner:

Instagram is focused on visuals

Instagram is basically for visuals. By visuals, it means that it uses videos, photos, and graphics only. They are the backbone of every marketer, and why many people are using Instagram as if it were the only social network available for business promotion, after all, it was patterned after Facebook. The gorgeous photos, videos, and graphics of your brand are the basic contents for a typical business account. This is one of the reasons people have selected a business account exclusively on Instagram. Captivating pictures of your product lure lots of buyers to you and even create more chain of followers. However, as mentioned before, there are other social platforms such as Facebook that enable features such as this, but Instagram outshines them because of the size of its number of users' base.

Access to Instagram Insights

With the fact that Instagram is uniquely created, it has lots of amazing insights which are only accessible to people with a business account only. A personal account is deprived of many things such as the insight provided for users of an Instagram profile. These insights are basic in-built-analytical tools. They are valuables that hint you on your followers, their appearance status, posts, likes, etc. Most of it all, you will be alerted on the posts of your followers and their reactions to them effortlessly. This is found on Instagram only. Every activity done by your followers and even their followers is part of what insights bring to you.

❖ Instagram Ads for business

Instagram is developed, as stated earlier, in Facebook way too. Therefore if you ever had an idea about ads on Facebook for businesses, you are on the right path to making an outstanding change on the Instagram platform. Meanwhile, the Ads on Instagram work in a quite different and effective way. About ads on Instagram, it enables you to track, set up and run campaigns. The campaigns are different activities on the platform aimed at reaching goals. Hope you remember how flooded the platform is and how prospective it will be in the future, pertaining to users. Instagram will give your business the popularity/awareness it deserves. The ads are specifically designed for businesses. You will activate it from your smartphones only, don't use a desktop for its effectiveness.

Contact button

For every person that owns a business account profile, contact button is enabled upon the view of your profile to allow potential buyers to contact you directly. Any form of business is entertained; all you have to do is to systematically design your bio to conform to Instagram. The contact button is not only for people to buy, but it is also used as a means of seeking support, inquiries or any other things relating to the business. With the selection of the contact button as well, you can receive Direct Message with the Instagram DM. The process of linking your about page is not discussed here, you learn it in other parts of this book. Instagram DM will allow you to reach out individually to some specific groups of people with a little space of time. Payment would have taken place even before much ado. You can as well receive reviews and commendation from clients.

❖ Links on Instagram Stories

This feature is only available to accounts that have been verified to enhance the operation of the account and even open it to diverse opportunities. Additionally, the account has to have a minimum of 10,000 followers in order to use this feature. In this book, you will learn ways of building your followers even from 0 followers to more than 10,000 followers. After you must have learned this, you should be open to the links to Instagram stories. With Instagram stories, you can be mentioned or commented on a story. For example, there is a link you clicked on the effect of drugs on humans' health, and you deal in the selling of the drugs, you will be able to give a comment while people contact you through your contact button. More so, people can mention you with specific Instagram outstanding features that will enhance your brand.

Chapter 4: Instagram Contents

As stated earlier, Instagram is a platform that works by visuals posts. Everything shared are either photos, graphics or videos. Because of this, very many people find it hard to create contents; many don't even know how to post or whether a posting is allowed. Those that know these are confused on what sort of content should be on Instagram. In this section, you will be taken through the parts of the content, types of contents and processes of creating content on Instagram. Attention is paid keenly to direct you through crafting perfect posts.

Because of the nature of the platform, visuals and branded storytelling are the keys of contents used. To engage your followers as a business-oriented person, telling a story about your product and services is the key to being the best seller. Posting pictures that are 'meaningless' will never add anything to your account. On Instagram, create a story that will be of great impact to your followers and any potential ones. The best thing to do is to put your gaze on your followers. You must, with utmost clarity, put them into consideration because they are the one to be engaged. Be adroit in your post to ensure entertainment and genuine contents. Be skillful in the way you arrange your photos. While uploading the photos, show them the nature of people in support of your business, the type of person you are, the muse of your story, and lots more. Don't take the time of your audience; make the story succinct and exclusive to Instagram news only. Be dynamic in the chronological arrangement of the stories. To ensure uniqueness of your profile, make sure you are updated on the latest trends on the platform. These trends could be news or hashtags, write on them and use them as well. Devise a way of connecting your interesting contents in such a way that your followers will have to stay on your profile to get the full story. Get the interaction with them interesting; they will surely look up for more. There are some basic things to consider while constructing a good Instagram content. These, according to Martins, are:

The Right time

You have to skillfully detect the right time to post your story based on your targeted audience. You must be up-to-date on their personal activities. Note that on your newsfeed, the most recent posts receive more attention which is why your post must be timely. You must key into an opportunity such as this. According to Martin "if your viral page is aimed at students who are online in the morning, then you should post in this period." This means the free time which your targeted audience is likely to be free to check their Instagram should be considered before posting. He gave another example that if you have 9-to5-jobbers as a target group, then you should write more posts after work. These people will have free time randomly; by this, you must post in their timing too. He, however, gave a recommendation which is not 'convenient test' as generally 7-9 clock (breakfast), 11-14 clock (lunch) and 17 to 20 clock (after work). The best interaction on Instagram was also given as 17-18 clock. The time frame of your location should not affect your audience consideration. Although most times, you and your followers are in the same meridian.

The Picture

Instagram can also be referred to as an electronic photo album. This is because it contains much of them. The pictures to be posted must be very attractive. Consider editing your photos before uploading them. Make sure the post is dynamic with different types of things such as comedy videos, photos and all. Try to upload pictures that are showing the practical time people are consuming your product. Research has it that many people consider photos from real life scenes of the product as the authenticity of the product. High-quality photos are recommended; make sure you don't post low-quality photos and videos. Be dynamic in the selection and arrangement of the pictures. Make sure you include a brand of your company on a photo that is not really related. Don't let your followers have bad impressions about you. If you make necklaces, consider using your friends as part of the models and then take their pictures for onward uploads on to your account. Take pictures of people that have worn the necklace to events such as weddings to authenticate it. Being outstanding should be your goal by creating compelling contents that entertain people. The type of pictures you will post for children will be different from the adults'. You must do all your best to get their target at different times as well. You should catch their attention at once sometimes too. The arrangement of your pictures also matters. The recommended arrangement is the grid formula. With a grid, you have the opportunity to arrange your pictures chronologically to explain the story you are telling. Apart from this, followers can quickly trace the story effortlessly. The posts must be able to hold anyone that runs across the posts; they must locate your account and follow.

The Text

Even though Instagram is basically visual, texts could be added to it sometimes too. Most times, these texts should be one that will require the action of the followers. The texts should vary between lengthy words and short ones. The place your company is located will be an additional text for you in cases you don't know the text to use. The aim is to engage your followers. Your text must be relevant to your pictures and most times should be one or two words. When you include your location, the post will be expanded to reach more audience thereby popularizing the account –this is your goal. Make sure the text is proofread, don't spoil the mind of the people that are already interested in you. Text can be a statement on the images uploaded as well. With this, if you are uploading pictures that are not a direct replica of your product, many of your followers will understand vividly.

Best steps to creating audience-centered contents

Having a business account requires the consistent engagement of your audience. This makes good contents an unavoidable thing to be included in your profile. You can consider the following tricks given by Instagram influencer Christina Galbato when creating a laudable content:

Use ready-made templates tools

When you want to create contents on Instagram and wonder how to create a pattern for them or perhaps stumbled on a great profile with nice and cool contents, and you want to create, template tools is what top Instagram influencers used. There are lots of tools Canva, Venngage and

Adobe with great Spark posts. These tools will craft an outstanding content that titillates the eyes and leave the mind wondering what sort the pictures is. You don't need to stress yourself, search for any of these tools, insert your pictures and you will be wowed by the outcome. It has trial sections, and you can equally choose manually that template you love.

❖ Research and Use High-quality stock images

That you will need lots of images is a fact. On the contrary, stock images could be awkward on your news-feed. Be extremely careful while using it most especially with templates. Everyone needs varying images to be created as contents, visit Stocksnap.io or Unsplash for free nice images. If you are buoyant enough, you could log onto Stocksy for images with high quality, different niche pictures, etc. Stocksy provides the greatest images because it is paid for and the developers want it to be worth it. Bear in mind that the standard pixel for images to be uploaded as content on Instagram is 1080p X 1080p to avoid automatic image resolutions. Stock images are always great and nice because the sites where they are found were actually developed to meet the criteria of social platforms such as Instagram.

Vary your content's format

Dynamism is the way forward in having a good followers' turn up on your content. You can't be deaf to the reaction of the followers when creating your contents. You could create a short video, say of 1-minute duration, explaining your product or showing the practical usage of your product. Don't bore your viewers with just a single type of pictures; it could be extremely boring really. A good Instagram profile will house varying contents. The distinction in the contents is only in their format. Take your time to create GIF contents as well. You could have a picture, GIF and short video and their permutation as well. This is what your audience is expecting, give them. Though Instagram takes both GIF and

Videos as the same thing, GIF is always shorter but interactive. Lots of people expect it as well. Stuff your contents with a variety of formats.

Search for brands within your niche and repost them

Perhaps creating contents yourself is barely possible because of time constraints. Don't worry; there is a way out of the tunnel. You can, with the consent of the writer, report a post within your niche from another content writer. Example of posts you could repost are those posts from fast-growing Instagram users. They must be of interest to your audience though. However, on Instagram, there are special steps to go through in order to make reposting official – reposting without proper consultation could lead to offense. Follow the steps below:

1. Follow hashtags and accounts to find out quality content

In order to validate your reposting, ensure that you have a similar audience and brand. Make the person you want repost his/her content is not a direct competitor to you. Make sure you have proper thinking on the content as well. You must follow the person in order to be updated on the posts of the person. To save the contents you would love to repost, try to create a collection for easy access. Searching for related contents through hashtag is also a legal way.

2. Contact the user for permission to repost

Before asking for permission, make sure you let the writer know they are doing a great job with proper credit and that your audience will be interested in the same post. To ask for permission, send the writer a DM through the arrow beneath the picture. Using the arrow has proven most efficient way, according to the report, of sending a direct message to account users.

3. Share the picture on your news feed

You can now share the picture to your feed once the permission has been granted. You must make sure proper credit is given to the source of the post anyway.

4. Save the Photo from Instagram or share directly through the repost feature

There are two ways of reposting on Instagram: saving from Instagram and reposting directly. For the first one, you will need to find the picture, click on the photo, double click it, view page source, type jpg there, copy the URL of the first option, open a new browser, paste it there, right click and save the picture. On the second option, copy the URL of the post you like and click on "repost" and it will automatically repost it. Note that the watermark is maintained when you use the second option. The first looks complex likewise, try to accompany the process given with required practical.

Create a UGC Campaign

The acronym UGC means 'User Generated Content.' It is used as content created by your followers. You could be the initiator, and they could post within your niche. This is also an activity similar to reposting of contents. User-generated content is typically contents crafted by any product user on their products without encouragement from anyone. These are contents solicited by you from your followers, though most times with incentives to encourage them. You can involve your followers in different ways: selling your product at a discount rate, conducting a competition on creating a post on your brand, etc. Instagram has suggested that you announce your hashtag even on other platforms especially the part of the incentives. Be strategic and dynamic in your request for contents from your audience. Without dynamism in your request, your feed will always be the same thing which will bore your audience. If you stipulate too many rules are guiding the kind of post you want, you might end up with no post as many people might be afraid they won't be considered. Relying too much on your followers is not a good idea as well. Make sure their posts are just supplementary and not the main thing. Proof to them you can actually create your content yourself and create a feeling that their support is a means to encourage them only.

Do influencer collaboration

One fantastic thing to do to create a good audience-centered profile is to work with other great brand promoters too. This will get you new followers, great feed and many other things enjoyed by the person you collaborated with. You must ensure the collaboration is with someone within your own niche to avoid exploitation and misunderstanding. Worry less on how to contact top influencers as many of them have a contact in their bio basically for collaboration inquiries purpose.

You have learned how to create good content for your brand and business. However, note that whatever means you are using to get your contents, designing will surely be done by you. Because of this, you will need to learn basic tricks used by top influencers to design their contents. These tricks are:

✓ Stating a precise focal point

While uploading your pictures and creating your format, make sure your photo has focus. The focus of photos means the center where you want your viewers to pay their attention only. If you create a picture with lots of images on, you might lose the focus, affecting its effect on the viewers. Therefore, put a single image with many other things, if need be, pointing only to the central idea of the photo.

✓ Adhere to the rule of thirds

The rule of thirds, found in photography, is all about arranging your interesting features along with a 9-grid picture intersection. This rule is a classic rule and executed by 9-grid photo imagination. Make sure that in uploading many pictures on your profile, you must adhere strictly to this rule —it is the secret of the top influencers. With amazing third rule obedience, you will adjust your grid to one-third of the picture you wish to upload as well.

✓ Create and apply white space and borders

Creating space and borders around your photos gives it a compelling look, and the audience will always want to gaze more. To avoid jam-packed uploads, ensure that you maintain some space between your third rule and focal point picture. Make sure you add this effect to all your posts, and you will experience rapid growth of followers.

✓ Rapt attention should be to Contrast and balance

Give your picture a good contrast while uploading. The contrast of your picture ranges over its color, light, shape, fonts, white space and border, and lots more. To ensure you have a perfect contrast setting, you could play around the various types of it on your Instagram app. Contrast is an important part of content designed to highly engage your audience. Many people are fascinated by the enhancement of a given picture even before focusing on the content itself. Contrast is like a finishing effect that 'crowns' your effort in content design. This is the last stage of content design, make sure it counts, and you will be amazed by the number of turn out your account will experience.

Chapter 5: Instagram Basic Features

The characteristics of Instagram as a social platform whose contents are in relation to visuals. Its premises on sharing and viewing graphics, videos, and photos. Its operations and plugins are categorized on its contents: visuals. The idea that it is used only by young people is very wrong. In this section, you will be guided systematically into the features of Instagram for either beginners or professionals. By beginners, it means people that are new to Instagram while professionals mean those familiar or even have an account on the platform. Some of the basic features with their operations include:

The filter options

While uploading pictures on Instagram, the filter is the section which enables you to add enhancements on the photos to be uploaded.

These filters make the pictures to look like studio edited ones. They are galvanized with features such as vintage, contrast, light, grayscale, soft glow, and lots more. Try uploading pictures and use this filter to create a special effect on them. Many influencers of Instagram claim that using these filters can make you outstanding among users of Instagram because the sense of filtration is typical only to you. Try it and grow your profile.

Like Button

One of the commonest features on Instagram is the like button. This platform can barely operate without features such as this. This is like an authorization given to fellow users to comment, follow or do anything to your post on the platform. The like button enables users to give either pleasing or unpleasing undertone remark on your posts. With the like button, lots of transformation like increment in the number of followers and the benefits that follow is activated.

The like button works in two places: it can be used on the home page, and it can be used as a user's dashboard. When the like button is used at the general page, it only gives remarks on the posts while when it is on the user's dashboard, the person becomes a 'follower.'

The Iconosquare feature

This is a form of a hashtag that is typically used to track campaigns. The performance report of the campaigns is what Iconosquare brings to you. You will be able to see relating data of the hashtag and even the growth alongside engagement of it on the campaign you have created.

The @ feature on Instagram

This is used basically for direct comment. This is for comment on posts on the platform. One could comment by tapping on the comment bubble through the person's username or type @ alongside the username.

The Word Suggestion content

This feature has been designed to help while typing on the platform. With a few words, you will be given any suggestion to make it easier for you to type. In the cases of comment, you will see related words while searching for a username. You will have related usernames.

Instagram set up operations

To download the Instagram app, one needs to consider the iOS of the medium to download it. If you have Android, you will download from 'Google Play.' If you have an iPhone, you will download from the 'App store.' Search these stores, you will, with ease, locate the app.

Registering your Instagram Account

After downloading the Instagram app, you will need to open an account. The app should create a 'shortcut icon' on your homepage after installation: if it didn't check your installed apps. Register your account or log in if you have an account already.

Creating your Instagram Account

Upon the location and clicking on the app, you will need to create a username and password. Your username can be any name combination. At this point your creativity is needed, the username can be a nickname. Care must be taken to use a name familiar to the people in order to facilitate the location and gaining of followers quickly. For example, you might consider using a clip of your first name and surname in uppercase or lowercase as 'TIMSAM' or 'timsam' for Timothy Samuel. After the username, use a password that is familiar with other platforms. You will surely need to add your email account which you could create one for the account. You can choose to add your phone number or not.

Uploading your profile photo

After you have created your account, as part of the process of perfect and strong Instagram account, you will need to add your profile picture. The picture can be taken immediately as you open your account but uploading an existing picture with high quality is highly recommended. Select 'Done' when you have uploaded the picture.

Friends and Family found on Instagram

For capitalization of your account to the full fledge, you will need to follow people that will share your pictures, and you do same to theirs. You can consider giving them your username or search from your account. With increment in followers, there are lots of benefits attached to it.

Adding and Following on Instagram

To be added to an account, you will be on the followers' list. You can follow and be followed respectively. Addition of a user will as well enable you to follow too. However, to randomly add people, you could click on the 'cog icon' on the home screen and click on 'invite friends.' With this, contacts of people around your vicinity will be suggested.

Connect to Social Media

You have an option on the app to search your phonebook directly. Simply click on 'My Contact,' and you will be prompted to search. Contacts with the Instagram account will come up, click on 'Follow' to add them to your account. Then, click on the home icon to return to the home of your account which should show the added accounts.

Home Screen

The icon looks like a house. It will automatically refresh itself when your photo has like, comment or when one of your friends add photos. The home will be updated with data, however.

Profile

The brief story created about you is your profile. The file card at the corner of the home screen contains your profile. Other things at this corner are photos, "following" and "Followers."

Privacy on Instagram

On the 'Edit my Profile' button, you can restrict the people that can view your profile. This is not encouraging, however, for a business person.

Privacy Off/on

When your privacy is turned off, anybody, even outside Instagram, can view your account. When it is switched on, only people following you can view your account.

News Feed

Photos, graphics, and videos are what is contained in the news feed. You can refresh the page by simply swiping it down. The news feeds are selected randomly; you scroll up or down.

Viewing comments from your Friends and family

The photo at the top left of your home screen is used to view people that have commented on your photo. Before clicking on it, there is something in grey color. It is meant to give you information about the comment.

Adding comment

Simply tap the speech bubble at the home screen which will prompt a new page to enable you to write your comment. Send it, and your name will appear right under the comment.

Attached Links

This feature enables people to be prompted to either another user's account or website. It is strategically attached to the account to enhance it. Most likely, it is a business account. If you click on surf new page, you can return to your home by tapping the back button on your phone.

The # Hashtag meaning

This feature is used to publicize a given post. By publicizing it, very many users will have access to the post. When you are using the hashtag, make sure there is no space between it and your post to avoid misunderstanding of your post. Additionally, when a hashtag is added to a post, it appears in blue. There are various reasons Instagram users use the hashtag. Some of these reasons include; promotion of business, gaining more followers, connecting to people that have the same idea and specialization as theirs, etc.

The hashtag enables you to search based on your specific interest on the platform. Your interest varies alongside many other things such as a book, mountain, etc. For instance, you could search with this #mountains. This will give you varying posts relating to your interest. Also, you will see profiles that have the same interest as you. The profiles that will be prompted will be top leading users who will teach you how best to construct your account too.

iOS, Android or Window icon

This particular icon is used to add photos. You can access it by clicking on the blue icon and then the circle at the bottom of the icon. Your gallery will be accessed automatically, and you can add your photo.

Followers icon

This is used to show the people that are following you in numbers. By followers, it simply means those people that your posts, whatsoever, will appear in their news feed. When you click on this icon, you will be able to see pictures of these people and either white color (to show you are following them) or blue button (to show you are yet to follow them).

Star symbols

This is technically referred to as the explore icon. It enables you to access a new page with a square at its top to type your information. With this icon, you can individualize your search. By individualizing, it means that you can search an account by hashtag or nickname. This facilitates a random and quick response from these people when you post. You can as well access their profiles upon searching.

Chapter 6: Building a strong Instagram Profile

Based on the fact that you are using Instagram as your marketing vendor, building a strong profile is the key to the success of any activity of a given account. A strong Instagram profile is one with many followers, posts, a growth of business and monetized account. This type of account is sorted for often times when people are searching on Instagram most likely because it is SEO optimized. Your account might have been existing or new, building a strong profile will, with few steps, create your dream – growing your business and brand. The importance of a good profile cannot be overemphasized in the process of growing and monetizing your personal account for your brand and business marketing. This is because it connects everything done on Instagram; your followers will be got through to you by a sound profile. Rapid growth is guaranteed with a sound and strong profile. Building a good business marketing is through a good profile as well. Monetizing your Instagram account which could generate thousands of dollars depending on your followers and account viewers is what you gain from business account profile. What is a strong profile? A strong profile is a profile with necessary bio, photos and a great number of followers. The greatness of a profile is subjected to factors such as those to be discussed here. With utmost clarity, the ideas the influencers used for their profile are discussed. While discussing all the secrets or hacks will be a herculean task, be sure that these steps are a conglomeration, with wide consideration, the ideas used.

Ever wondered how some people have followers to the extent of being renowned for it? It is to the extreme of you following the person – who was only searching for a way to get followers too. One of the things according to psychologists that appeal and cannot elude the human brain is a beauty. Many say beauty is in the eyes of the beholder, but the question is: what constitute the beautiful ones in the eyes of the beholder? Things are not coincidental as many people assume! This boils down to the fact that the person has created some sensations in you that stimulated you even unconsciously. Well, this is the aim of the account user. The account user must be using a secret or hack that is quite exceptional which could be learned on a platform like this book. The end of frustration of getting your desired goals for creating an Instagram profile is right in this book. The user has systematically built a strong profile whose effects cannot be shunned. Instagram is not just as a general social network. If you have a personal account, it will be better you create a business one. Reason being that the features specified to achieve your goal (growing and monetizing through marketing) barely work on the personal account. Make sure you have optimized everything you wish to do on Instagram. Do not leave your profile empty as people could actually search for you. How do you build a strong profile? Below are a few steps to building a strong Instagram profile, viz:

Download and Install an Instagram App

While many people prefer to operate their Instagram profile through their lap/desktop, to create a strong business-oriented account, you will need to download the smartphones version. The reasons for this will become clearer as we continue. Many phones come with an Instagram app installed in them. However, some don't, therefore, go to play store search for it, download and install.

Create an account without business infiltration

After downloading and installing the app, creating an account that is not related to business is the next thing to do. Note that from the inception of Instagram in 2010, it was designed for social relations only, but few users found more to it which even made developers of the app include the business plugin on it in subsequent versions. For a strong profile, you will need to start your account without business plugins. Open the app and select the option 'create an account.' After you have done that, the next thing is to upload a profile picture of you.

Use or upload a photo of your real self or relating to you only (in such as a business account)

Basically, on Instagram, much things done are through or relating to posting pictures. Getting a vibrant picture is high. Make sure you use pictures that will project clearly its details. The picture you must use in building a strong profile must be you or relating to you. It is necessary because most people that will be following you must be able to recognize you as many people to follow people randomly –they need to know the person. If you use any photo, you are weakening the chance of a strong profile. In the case of a business profile, the strongly recommended one, you must be sure you use your logo on any picture you are using or uploading. Not only will using your photo or logo help you with a strong profile, it will make people familiarize themselves to them most especially in cases where they don't know you but got fascinated by the pictures.

Consistency matters because when you have people that comment or mention you, it will make it clearer upon your reply and you will get many people to follow you as well. Use consistent and high-quality pictures to start a step to your strong profile. Note that first impression matters while building a strong profile —this is from your pictures.

Using a recognizable or SEO optimized username

While opening an account on Instagram, it is not enough to have a username randomly. It is rather nice to make sure that the username is SEO optimized and searchable for anybody. Getting that name combination is always good, but it is never enough. That big profile you can see must have rested on this username hack. To build a strong profile, details such as this, which are not taken to consideration by most people need to be done by serious-minded business-oriented ones. A username is a word in lowercase as your identity on the platform. It is what people use to mention and tag other users too. For example, https://instagram.com/jennyjay is a URL of Jennyjay's account which can be used during Ad's on or any link to the profile. The username, though need familiarity with the world, needs to be unique to some degree. You might not be the only with such username, but uniqueness matters. However, use less of symbols to facilitate your strong profile.

It is pertinent to note that as wonderful as it is to have a good username, be careful when you consider changing your username. Perhaps, you have had an account before encountering this book, you are strong to advise to maintain your username or if need be, open a new account with the knowledge you have gained. It is important because once people comment your username, it stores on the platform to the extent that every post shared goes with it. Then, if you change your username, you will need to get all the posts you have a comment on or mentioned to change the name as well. Note that the traffic you generate is part of what is considered in the process of monetizing your account. This is one of the secrets according to tailwindapp, an account with 428 thousand followers that facilitate your strong profile. It is related to your business name and logo too. It could be sad, but the truth is that even blog posts, articles, and everywhere the username has been to will have to keep up to maintain the standard. The start of a strong profile is from a good and standard username selected. When you are choosing, you can consider including your "native or nickname" that is exclusive to you. Good username, great profile!

Select a meaningful and searchable name

This is very different from the username. Meanwhile, people can use it to search. Your name can be edited any time perhaps the situation requires it. To build a strong profile, having a good optimized name enhances the popularity of the account. The name is what people see on your bio. It could include such a thing as "AMRAP Life | Active Wear." While there is quite a range of keywords you will use for your name, use the words pertaining to your business. A test could be to search, before selecting the name, for the name and see how people will locate you. Make it simple and meaningful. Think what people will think of searching for the kind of business you are doing, surround your name around their 'assumed' thoughts —humans are less predictable anyway. With a searchable name in your profile, you are building a strong profile already. Information is always simple and unbelievable because of the means of gathering them. Be assured that this is a vital measure used by those influencers you could see on Instagram. Good name, a wonderful and strong profile is guaranteed. Unlike the username, the name chosen can be changed without changing it from anywhere it has been mentioned or commented. You can decide to change your name any time once its keywords are optimized. The great name creates a strong profile.

Construct/ craft an attractive Bio for your Instagram

It is about time to construct an amazing bio. What is Instagram Bio? It is a group of about 150 words telling people about who you are and chiefly, why they should follow. This bio needs to be crafted strategically to depict the exact business brand you are using. It must be highly succinct and maximized to catch the attention of the viewers even from a glance. It is an opportunity to captivate and engage your viewers with what you have on your profile. You don't have to be confused concerning what you can do or what you love doing so that the profile will be gorgeous. Perhaps, you consult a friend to give you a simple analysis. The language must be easy to relate with and not too much grammar. You have to sandwich emoticons readily provided for you in the construction of your bio to make it easier and attractive to read.

In the words of tailwind, one of the most Instagram influencers in 2017, the following are suggested formats of a good Instagram Bio. They are:

➢ Write your bio in an online character counter to keep it to 150 characters or less. Use an emoji dictionary to make sure you choose universal emojis: This means that for an effective Bio, one needs to make sure it is in the optimized version of what people do on other social platforms, say,

Whatsapp. This is because there is a connection between your account and them and people can easily make reference to you. The emoji will add flavor to the reading in order to save people of the thought of another reading —it is a social media, not a classroom lecture!

➢ Add in line breaks where needed: Lots of space can enhance the look of your bio. This will make it more attractive, unique and decent. Make sure you apply it.

➢ Copy and paste to your Instagram bio on your desktop. Whenever you are copying from an online character counter tool, try pasting into Notes, Notepad, Evernote, or even a Facebook status update before you paste it to your profile on Instagram: This will create a nice and standard format for your bio. If you typed directly from Instagram, the view from the public would never look vibrant. In fact, sometimes, the emojis will lump together like queues in the bank. You must have noticed lots of accounts that are flooded with posts, format and all; this is their secret as Tailwind revealed in his blog post. It is worthy of emulation.

Create a nice grid with at least 9 pictures:

According to smart, one of the best ways to build a strong profile is to create a grid view of your pictures. These pictures must be of very high quality in order to enhance the effect. The least of pictures should be like 9 pieces neatly arranged in a chronological manner to engage a potential follower. You don't have to panic concerning whether your new pictures will be of interest to your followers or potential followers. The effect of a grid photo will enhance your posts with less dislike and even gain more followers. The grid will as well lead the followers to view and know more from your profile. Having created a nice and attractive bio, username and photo, the potential will either follow you or in some other cases refer to you when your services are needed in other posts. A good photo gird will beautify your account. A strong profile is coming up already. Make sure all pictures are of you and/ have the logo of your brand. There are times that followers download posts from Instagram which go viral. With this, your brand name is moving to the next level. You are assuming that position already. Use your best pictures for a start, abstain from a clumsy grid. Make it simple and short. It is yours, be very creative with it.

- Make sure you select a business category in your account

A business category is what is or closes proximally to your business. It is necessary because many people are after product or services which must be stated in your profile as they visit it. It is nothing special, but its impact can't be eluded. While searching on the platform through products and services, it helps you get closer for selection. The category specification is one of the funniest things people shun while creating a profile on Instagram. Take your time while opening the account, do the necessary, remember that this is part of your career and business. This category selection is best-selected on the smartphone and not the desktop or laptop – its potency is generated by these phones because they have been specifically designed for it. Perhaps you don't need a direct correlation of your business, select that which is closely related to it. Amazingly, once you select one category while searching the site, closely or related business comes up which enables potential followers leading to the popularity or awareness of the brand. This will lead to a strong profile.

Add contact options to your profile

For your strong profile, make sure you add a means of contact to your bio. The basic reason being that while some people are only dormant follower whose aim is to enjoy the muse got from your profile, most of the followers have interest in your our business, and so, they will like to contact you directly for business. Without a contract, according to the site, many users take the account as unserious. Once the aim of your profile is business-driven, then do the needful by adding a means of contact. The contact could be mail, phone number or any other social platform username. However, most people take mail as the official means of contact when it comes to business. Use your mail or at least your mobile number. Make sure your profile is great. The process of adding a contact is done through your smartphone.

- Convert your account to a business one

After creating every bit of your account to suit a business profile, switching your account to business one is the next thing to perfecting your strong profile. To start with this, try to create a business account Facebook account.

Perhaps you have one, and then the process is simpler now. Log in to your Instagram account, go to menu settings at the top right corner. This button is basically iOS or ellipsis on an Android. Move down the menu settings selected, select the option "Try Instagram Business tools," you should be prompted to connect your account to the Facebook Business created. After this, Instagram will pop up a message on whether it should manage your Facebook Business account, select 'Yes' and your accounts are connected already. Your business account profile is ready.

Create and use your bio Instagram link

Very many Instagram users use just one link which is from their bio. Hope how to create an attractive bio learned earlier in this chapter is intact? if not, revise it. If you don't use your link, it will be traffic for Google, and while monetizing your account, Google would have had the details.

Chapter 7: Growing your Fan Base

Since the growth of Instagram as a social platform, many business runners have gone there to grow and promote their brands. The change in the policy of Facebook in the wee of 2015 was part of what skyrocketed mass movement to Instagram. Instagram has grown to the extent of having over 800 million active users; the number of Instagram users have increased to over 1 billion too. Though Instagram was fashioned like Facebook, its prowess is on how it has, within a short period of invention, grown much more members. About 80% of Instagram users operate a business account. Do you wonder how a platform that started typically as photo uploads has become a marketing ground for all and sundry? The secret is simple; many started by growing their fan base. A fan base is the number of the audience gathered or following your account. As a starter, you must learn some tips on how to grow your fan base. The importance of having a fan base is huge. It could get you more clients for your business, monetize your account, popularize your brand and many more. In this section, you, either a starter or a growing starter, will learn how to manage and grow your fan base. Below are tips for you:

Create and post extremely creative contents

Influence of Creative contents on your brand is very much. Many Instagram users with great fan base use this trick to attract many followers. Those that have enough fan base are even craving more —it is very competitive, you can't afford to be creative. With a creative content, you will earn more comments, likes and eventually followers. Abstain from posting silly-willy, make sure everything counts. Create stories with your posts and arrange them in chronological order to suit your targeted audience. Most importantly, consider your niche and craft a story about it.

Make sure you give your audience enough suspense with your contents. Don't forget that everything is visual. Create your stories and arrange them in a chronological order to suit and boost the curiosity in your audience.

Consistent posting

Over the years, Tailwind, a prolific Instagram analyst reported studying the growth of Instagram users has been a result of their posting. From 2017 reports, users that posted consistently experienced much more followers and likes. After the curiosity of your audience has been created, consistent posting is the key to keep them. With more carefulness, systematic posting based on the kind of story and reactions of your audience is crucial. You will have to post at least once in a post. Note that results of your posts will increase with much patience -don't expect deus ex machina.

Using the right Hashtag

Hashtags are used to capture people even outside your followers. If you want your fan base to grow, using the right hashtags will get your post to everyone within your niche. With hashtags, you are assured that every Instagram user will get your content and invariably follow your account. One of the things you should take note of is how specific your hashtags are. Don't use hashtags that will house some other ones in them. This will not create what you want: reaching a large audience. Rather, other related posts will be suggested alongside yours. But with a specific hashtag, you could have only your post a suggestion to your followers and to those who are not following you. For example, if your niche is on handmade diamond pedals Necklace made in Mexico, make a hashtag on #handmadeMexicanDiamondPedalsNecklace and not something like #handmadeNecklace as it will be opened to lots of suggestions. Your focus on using a variant hashtag is very important as well. Make sure that they are trending things going viral around the Instagram community as many people will be searching within that time for such thing. Many Instagram influencers rest on such trending things, though transient, to grow their fan base. Actually, the number of hashtags permitted to be used on Instagram for a single post is 30. Using hashtags and their number is a bone of departure among Instagram users, many of them recommended using just nine for a single post.

Influence your Followers to be a good content creator

Creating good content is very good and fine but that you might be stranded at some point is a fact. Instead of creating and posting all by yourself all the time, you can involve your followers in the creating of contents. Try and create contents that will make your followers create brand content for your business as well. You might need to divert your attention from your brand to your followers. In the account of Buffer, a top leading Instagrammer with huge fan base growth through followers' content creating, witnessed a huge increment of 400% using this method. This will even encourage your followers to post contents relating to your brand and business. Imagine you have 10, 000 followers and at least 5,000 of them create a single post for your brand –this is a great method proven to grow your fan base.

Conduct Contests

Organization of contests is another fantastic way of growing fan base. This is because people's attention will be drawn solely to your account for what they stand to get upon following your account. Be calculative in your thinking; create contents that will promote your brand itself. Makeup contests that will give you fantastic ideas on your brand. Make them mention you in comments to increase your visibility, repost your previous contents and lots more. Many followers were recorded for Graphix who devotes much time in to contest creation such as "win a trip to Fiji." You can as well make your followers create similar content for your brand. Note that what your brand needs at the moment should be your contest. With this, you will witness a consistent, rapid growth of your fan base on Instagram. With a good fan base, your brand will witness a good marketing size and even sales. In fact in the case of Earphix's win a trip to Fiji contest, there was a response rate of 10,000 comments. This is huge; you can get the same testimony.

Influencers' collaboration

Checkup Instagrammers with a good number of followers. Contact them to approve your brand as well. Make sure you contact people within your niche as people will not consider a request from outside their scope. Your request is basically on how you can feature on their page. You could create a promo on your brand and tell the person to mention it on their page. When your name is mentioned, be assured that their fan base will get your posts as they look out for them. This is somehow perceived in doing great influence on your fan base. The user can as well tag you in their post. Contacting a social media expert to use and post content relating to your brand will also grow your fan base. A turn up of 10,000 followers with a single collaboration is guaranteed.

Posting at relatively different times of the day

A new strategy developed lately is posting at diverse time of the day. It is not enough to create and post contents, considering appropriate time will grow your fan base rapidly. On a report from the Sprout Social, the accurate times to post content should be from Tuesday of the week to Friday of the same. And that, to witness huge audience engagement, it should be published between 9 am and 6 pm each day. They gave a recommendation to Thursday posting, however.

They gave the order of their posting as 5 am to 11 am with 3 pm to 4 pm on Thursday while other days like Wednesday and Friday should be 3 pm and 5 am respectively. While these timings might not suit you all the time, create a schedule for your post within this range and see what effect it has on your fan base. This timing has, however, proven by reports, to be a workable one. Take this as an opportunity and grow your fan base.

Advertising on Instagram

Advertising on Instagram is very easy and rewarding. This is because Instagram contains some ads that enable you to advertise with ease on Instagram. With these ads, many of your followers will notice no difference in your normal posts and the advertisement. The ads available for you are slideshows, videos, photos, and carousels.

Slideshow ad is a combination of pictures of your brand with a piece of underground music added to it. The pictures are usually 10 and tell a story about your brand. The format of this ad is different from the video, and thus, people can easily load it.

Video and photo ads have no special features except your sponsor label is attached at the topmost part of them. They are the normal posts on your account. They contain different types of audience engagement.

Carousel ad is basically for combining different types of your post into a single advert. Make sure you select posts that have a subsequent huge number of followers and comments. For the initial followers will get alert on the post, they have either commented or followed.

Because of the effect of these ads on the growth of fan base, Instagram developers have recently created the view for story highlight for brand and business. To experience a huge effect as make sure you vary your ads to see which is most effective for you. Ads will give your product the publicity it deserves. With them, you could analyze the kind of people interested in your posts and eventually, brand. After noticing these people, the strength of your post will be out and you will know how to involve everyone.

Using Geo-tags in your posts

Geo-tag, as its name suggests, is used for geographical location. With good geo-tag, followers will be able to locate where your company is. The effect of this is that, when your service is needed, people will know where to contact you. If peradventure your followers are in a place where your brand is needed, you will get an adequate recommendation. According to a report, using geo-tags could increase your brand by 79% within a short period of time. Good publicity is got from using your geo-tags. When encouraging your followers to create contents, try telling them to include the location of your office as well. This will increase the growth of your fan base and even your sales. Everywhere will be stormed with your brand.

Use captions to engage your audience

Posting to engage your followers is very important, but its effect on your audience can barely be measured. To grow your brand, try to use appropriate captions like emojis, trending slangs, trending situations around, etc., while posting. This is a means to get quick comments and feedback from your followers. When people comment on your posts, their followers get to know about it especially if it is based on the latest trends in town. Using a mixture of emojis on a post that is contrary to it could spring up lots of feelings from your audience, hence, their comments. With a good and timely caption, you are guaranteed good feedback from your followers. If you post a content ending with a question mark, for example, varying answers from your followers will lead to a very long talk and interactions on your post, thereby promoting your fan base. Even though Instagram is not a chatting social platform, you could solicit for how your followers are faring with captions. With this, many of your followers will feel loved and reach out for your posts often. Abstain from using an automatic response to comments on your posts. Try to respond and appreciate every comment on your post. This will go a long way. There are some cases where what people say about your post is contempt. Be very careful in your response to such comments. Don't let the judgment affect your post. Be polite at every point, knowing fully well that the critique is not the only person following you.

Always like photos within your Niche as well

A good student makes a good teacher. A good follower makes a good Instagrammer. Make sure you go through other Instagram influencers within your brand and like at least 10 of their posts. Dropping encouraging comments and checking through their tags is a great way to grow your fan base as well. Growing a good fan base is not all about getting followers but rather being a follower as well. Look for top fan base accounts and like them. Spend enough time on their profile. Don't do spam, be simple in your approach. If you are, sometimes when they don't have a particular product, you could be recommended. Well, it could be the law of karma working right here. Do to others what you expect them to do to you.

Devise a good theme for your photos

When people's expectation has risen, it must be fulfilled. This is why you can't afford to create your posts anyhow, rather use nice themes. This strategy is the aftermath of sourcing for followers. When you have tried every style to have a fan base, consider improving your themes while uploading. It is a great way to grow your fan base.

Always drop comments

While going through posts on the news feed, respond to them. Don't forget that Instagram is a social platform as well. Learn to socialize. By doing this, you are publicizing your brand as well as growing your fan base. It is never a waste of time to comment randomly on news feed.

Create and encourage hashtags

As an originator of popular hashtags, you stand a chance of getting enough fan base. Many people want to grow their fan base by using trending hashtags; thus, they search for them and invariably promote the creator. Always encourage your followers to use this hashtag as well because the more their post grows, the better for the hashtag (you as well). You can create a nice hashtag from your photos that will attract a great number of followers as well.

Connect your account to other social networks

Attaching your Instagram username to your Facebook, Blog and Twitter posts could earn you a great fan base. Don't make an assumption on whether your readers and friends on these other platforms are following you. You could create a photo telling them to like your post. This will increase the number of followers you get in return.

Conduct a diagnostic test on your posts

This a simple way of growing your fan base. You will scan through all your posts and get those with great likes and build your subsequent posts on them. By detecting your audience's likes, you can create a good post that will be of better concern to your followers. If you notice a form of declension on the number of likes you have, find out by scrutinizing the strength and weakness of your posts compared to the initial ones. Stay away from posts with lesser likes, check their themes and their looks and improve on them.

Chapter 8: Converting Followers into Clients via Instagram Sale Funnel

Getting enough followers is very crucial to a business account. Likewise, having a good number of engaging followers, it very key to any given account. However, the serendipity of harnessing followers to potential clients is another story. The conversion of followers to clients is a great concern to every brand and product developer. This is because after undergoing rigorous acts of compiling enough followers, the aim is to maintain or step up the sale. No business builder will do things that will harm the business —divided attention could actually do some malignity to business. After getting enough followers with the aim of improving sales which in the long run is turning to waste of time and effort, how does one convert followers to clients? This is a question of great concern. What are followers without sales? These and many more questions are what come to your mind. Don't worry. You will be taken through some strategic processes whereby you can, through your Instagram sale funnel, make a sale directly on Instagram.

Lately, because of the increase in the number of people using Instagram for business, the developers have included what is called Shopping Instagram. This is a plugin on the site that enables one to make a sale, i.e., convert followers into potential buyers. This plugin, however, is basically made available for American users. To operate this shopping Instagram feature, you need to have a Facebook Shopping setup and Facebook Business page. As the features seem exclusive to a particular group of people, selling through the Instagram funnel is the way out. It is pertinent to consider the fact that conversion here means the ability to interact with followers to become clients. Additionally, the attention of this book has been shifted from discussing gaining followers to the sale funnel and the followers. In other words, the conversion of followers will be discussed from the point of view of the channel through which the conversion is made –Instagram sale funnel.

Therefore, Instagram sale funnel is the stage in which a company puts its buyers through the selling-buying process. These are the phases of sales taken by a company. Even though the term looks vague, resting solely on the meaning of it will solve a great percentage of the problem. In short, Instagram sale funnel is the phase-by-phase process buyers are taken through by a company during the transaction on Instagram. There are over 700million Instagram users that have been using this means as a sale medium. Yours will not be the first. Because of this, there are, of course, different strategies employed by these people while converting their followers to potential buyers. These secrets will be divulged here.

According to Instagram reports, the first thing to bear in mind before converting followers into buyers is the relationship established with the followers. As a user on Instagram, you have to consider creating a long-term relationship with your followers. This is part of the reasons for not creating a note of spam or scam while contacting top Instagram influencers. With a good relationship, interaction is made easy: conversion is made easy. In the first stages of your growth, how did you contact your followers and how often have you been engaging them? If your answers are encouraging and nice, a good percentage of the problem is solved. Get to your followers and try to implement some or all of the following steps (remember discussions are given based on sale funnel):

➢ The highest point/top of the Funnel

On the hierarchical organization of the funnel, the top part consists of the followers on your account. These are the people you have, with steps since the inception of this book, gathered as your followers. They are the people within your niche. The more people you have in your funnel right here, the better for you as they will be the ones to be converted to your clients. You will learn how to grow your Instagram followers in the subsequent chapter. Make sure you apply them where appropriate. On the status of conversion, the general conversion rate is at 3 which is based on the number of people who have visited your profile for onward actions such as appending a lead form on Instagram. The more people you get to visit your site through your Instagram account, the better your conversion rate. If you, for example, have 10,000 followers and all of them could take the action of filling out a lead form on your site, you will have at least 3,000 sales from Instagram. People that have grown their followers through automated machine should take note as the generated followers are not real and thus will not be of help on a sale conversion rate. This is why it is recommended to build your followers in a legal way as it will, in turn, help you along the line of your business and brand growth. Getting followers, as a point of reminder, can be fast by; using necessary hash and geotags, conducting a contest, telling stories, using grid format, using feeds themes, etc. Whatever means (apart from using machines) you have or will use to grow your followers, the main thing is to fill up the top of your funnel –it is the space for your followers.

Centre or Mid of Funnel

Growing and filling up the topmost part of the funnel is fine and good. Having consistent engagement from your followers is what brings increment in the sale on Instagram. The middle part of the funnel comprises followers that consistently comment or like your posts on Instagram. They are the direct receiver of your contents. They constitute the yardstick for judging your contents and post. At this stage, what will help your sale is how you have been interacting with your followers on sales and why people should buy from you. If this had been in place, you would be able to convert your followers in top buyers/clients. In fact, your conversion rate might increase above 4% within a few days with a good interaction among your followers. Giveaway contest and asking your followers for opinion is a huge tactic for getting your followers' involvement in your post.

Apparently, good and strategic contents create lots of interactions amongst followers. Anyone that needs the interaction of their followers should develop audience-centered contents. The processes of designing and creating good content have been discussed in the previous chapter, revise before continuing. Interestingly, in order to attain the fullest of timing and days of posting to catch the interaction of your audience, you can create your content and use a platform such as Sprout to schedule when your content will be posted on your news feed. This, unlike the bot used to generate followers, does not have any influence on your sales on Instagram. Therefore, you should be busy, use these sites to schedule your contents. You will be able to convert your interactive followers into a good sale on Instagram. If you don't have enough active followers, consider applying the steps given, and you will experience a magical change in your middle funnel. Take your account to the next level you desire.

The low part of the Funnel

These are the people who you are conversant of as your followers. They are people who have visited your site through Instagram. They might have made a purchase of your brand actually, and they are very used to you. They're never motivated to comment or like your post. They can be referred to as the permanent followers on your Instagram. When you are redirecting followers from your Instagram to other sites, make sure there is a correlation between the landing page and the content viewed. This is important for the times you are creating stories with your contents on Instagram. You don't have a problem with a funnel at the bottom as they are willing to buy your brand and even promote it when necessary. Meanwhile, link to redirect is not made available for every post; you will need to put hashtag for your followers to click on your bio. Invariably, you might want to use a customized URL on your bio; this is fine and effective too. There are different means of getting URL such as generating through google or buying from other domain sellers –this is expensive though.

The conversion of your followers to clients stages have been discovered alongside the phases of Instagram sale funnel. There is no magic actually, and not everyone that follows you is willing to buy your product, don't be heartbroken. Make sure you are always right at every point of your interaction. This will go a very long way in helping you to grow to make fine sales through your Instagram. Always change, when necessary, the link in your bio to reflect the latest post, especially when you are telling stories. Build good followers with the initial aim of making them your permanent clients.

Chapter 9: The road to getting 20,000 followers on Instagram

That brands and businesses get enough exposure is a fact on Instagram. Many people are there to market their brands, so are you! It is actually not enough to market without followers. It is very easy to open an account, post photos and all –getting audience never comes easy. For marketing on Instagram, you have to work tenaciously to get your own followers. One of the reasons it is difficult to get a loyal audience is lack of the ability to catch and hold their attention. The opportunities that await a profile with a reasonable number of followers are much –why many are after the growth of their followers. To get enough audience, you have to be consistent as in 2016, Instagram has changed the operation of Algorithm and as such, the old time way of doing things has changed. Many people, because of this, have decided to get shout out from top influencers which are very expensive – especially when they know what it is used for. You don't have to search for other options asides the ones to be given here. It is a compilation of what these top influencers have been engaging to get and retain their followers. The importance of followers coupled with the task of getting them necessitated this section. Here, you will learn, with a practical step-by-step guide, road to getting 20,000 followers. Don't ever think it will come easily. Everything lies in consistency and strategy. If one of your strategies is not yielding, consider changing it based on the report you must have got through your post likes. To enhance the learning and effectiveness of these steps, they have been divided into batches ranging from 0-100, 100-1000, to 5,000, 10,000 and then 20,000 and above. Less panic on how you can grow your followers to at least 20,000 followers; here are steps gathered from top Instagram influencers:

☐ Growing your followers from 0 to 100

For a start, you will have less problem getting or building your first 100 followers because you have had your community. Against this, you might consider sending a newsletter to your friends and family. Make sure you plan very well in the way you invite people. Actually, most of the time people give out their username to everyone known. If you have a good number of the community which could be because of your behavior, growing your first 100 followers should not be hectic. Be a good judge of your post. Very many people take this stage as growth without posts since the people you want are basically followers got 'manually.' Recommendation on at least getting one post is advisable. This is because this post will not only start as bedrock in your portfolio but also a judge on how people respond to your brand. If you are an existing brand that needs only promotion, asking your loyal clients to follow you on Instagram will go a long way. In the same vein, discounting your product for the first 100 people is a recommended idea. People don't work where they don't earn, so putting your discount say the first 10 people get 100% discount, first 50 gets 50% discount, and so on; so as to carry everyone along without ill feelings. When you send in your invitation, make sure you have something to offer them —which is why having your first post is crucial. The invitation could be in the form of an announcement like whether something novel is coming at hand. Before the announcement as well, get a very great bio which contains website for onward visitation. In the description of your bio, make it brand-centered, use emojis where necessary and write catchy contents for your audience. Apart from looking for followers, you can as well be a follower. When you log into your account, search for people within the niche of your brand and business, follow them and begin your product publicity. Setting your account and looking for followers will not get you a quick response. Instead, be on the two sides of the line and move your account forward with great followers.

Interacting with the account, you have decided to follow will earn your followers as well. Like the post of the top people within your niche, drop your comment on their recent posts or send them a single sentence DM on how you would love to have them as your follower. It is pertinent to consider the number of followers of the account you want to follow -10,000-50,000 followers is highly recommended. Make sure you consistently converse with these followers, so as to show some signs of seriousness.

There is another way to getting your followers; perhaps you don't have an announcement or community of friends. With this strategy, you will have to develop much of your news feed through fantastic posts. Having a post within 9 to 12 coherent grid will be enough before reaching out to 'external' followers. In the previous chapter, you have been taught how to design contents and chiefly sites that could generate a nice grid for your photos, take advantage of this and make the best out of your brand. Many followers, according to top Instagram influencers, love or get carried away by a fantastic grid. Leverage on this, create your brand photos; in fact, many people think you take your product more seriously with a good photo grid. Posting like 12 contents in a day is cool, but many influencers recommended posting them within 2 to 3 days to enhance your account publicity. Don't be too anxious to post all in a day. On the usage of hashtags, stuck your post with lots of hashtags so that you can get your contents as feed to a wide range of people. Bear in mind that using too many tags could debar your posts from getting to the targeted audience accurately. For your easy consumption, Hopper gave the following steps in summary:

☐   Create an interactive bio with an incentive to follow –an offer, the posts themselves or both;

☐   Engage with people and brands that might be interested in your contents on a regular basis;

☐   Work on your first posts to develop your own style;

☐   Research more and less popular hashtags, pick out as many relevant ones as you can, and use them on your posts.

Growing your followers from 100 to 1,000

One of the greatest challenges is to start your growing of follower; working on it becomes easy. After you have got 100 followers, moving to the badge of 1,000 is the next target. You are on the right path if you have implemented the first strategies given to you. Here are a few tips that could help you grow your followers:

Identification of top Instagram influencers

Here, like part of the strategies given in the initial stage of growth, search for people with 50000 followers, and follow them. Don't hesitate to comment on their posts nor like their recent contents. This will enable them to like and take a special interest in you too. You could decide to add enough comments on posts you noticed their followers had given less concern. This will make you stand out among them. Of course, the accounts you are following and liking are those within your niche or similar to your products and brand.

Analyzing how realistic their followers are

At the tail end of this book, you will be taught how to generate followers using some designed Instagram automated tools. The work of these tools is to get, either real or machines enough followers for your account. Because of these tools, you might need to cross-vindicate the type of followers on the account you are following. Real life followers could create lots of growth in your account as they could, upon noticing you, follow you as well. Wondering how on earth you will do this analysis? Fewer worries, technology has made life better. Use socialAuditpro or

Fameaudit for your analysis. They have proven to be the best amongst others. You could source for related ones too; it is a free world.

Following the real Followers

After you have generated and analyzed the real Followers from the accounts you will like to follow, consider following the followers with a real image at the expense of cartoon or logo profile pictures. When you are done following them, sit back at your own account and try to get those accounts that are following you and those that are not. Unfollow accounts that are not following you because of Instagram's algorithm premise on the healthy mutual following. You must get at least 20% of your followed accounts to follow you. Don't be sad about unfollowing people. There are lots of people to follow within your niche. Holding accounts that won't follow you is a Trojan to your growth. Likewise, there are lots of apps both in iOS and Android formats that help in denoting followers that don't follow you back, search for them and incorporate them into your account.

It is never enough to put the blame on those that don't follow you; you could be the cause of such action. Many people follow accounts that have a great number of followers, a well-crafted feed, real account picture and have lots of followers than it is following. Additionally, you can switch on the posting notification for these accounts so that you will be the first person to drop a nice comment on their post. You have to be creative in the way you drop your comments, dropping normal comments like, "Great" or "Impressive" can't be special.

One of the landmark tricks to 1,000 followers is to add the times taught in the previous chapter on schedules for posting. You have to organize your posts now. Posting when you 'feel like' posting might not help an account with 1000 followers. On your adventurous road to 1000 followers, applying both following and unfollowing tricks are recommended for you.

Growing your followers from 1000 Followers to 5000 Followers

At this stage, you are already becoming an expert, and so, you have to be more creative than before. You have learned the basics of growing your followers. At this point, you are using a combination of the initial strategies and the ones to be given here. Funnily, you might have got over 5000 followers. You will surely need these tips because those that follow you can equally unfollow you. Here are a few things to do:

Usage of Engagement groups

Like every other social media platform such as Telegram, Instagram has engagement groups. These are groups of people within a niche and are willing to comment, follow and like one another's posting. They are interacting with one and another continuously. However, many of Instagram engagement groups have their mode of operation, some permits like only, some comments, etc. depending on their agreed rules. It will be better if you abide by the rules. The times for posting are always announced as well, take note of this. To post such a username, it is usually 30 minutes intervals. There are times where interaction happens 30 minutes before approval of whatever postings. Get enough engagement groups on your postings; make sure you have lots of them for normal interaction. Though getting too many engagements at the initial stage is not encouraged, follow the timing of growth. It is a crucial factor in growing.

However, Instagram has from 2017 changed its algorithm. As of 2016, people post with hashtags of famous people. If these famous people like your post, the frequency of your appearance on the feed will be boosted. Unfortunately, this doesn't work anymore. What works now is group engagement. It could be temporal too but leveraging on it to build your account is not a bad idea either. To get these groups, you can search for them on Google or tell someone on the group to add you. Some scammers are right here for you. They claim that there is an entrance fee for your intended groups. Beware.

Invest more on Instagram ads

For everyone building brand and business on Instagram, getting your hands on ads on Instagram is very crucial. You have been taught different types of ads and where to get them in the previous chapters. Try to review them and apply accordingly. Take advantage of ads; they will grow your followers rapidly. In order to lay hold of your ads on your account, follow the following:

- Log in to your account
- Click on your profile
- Go to your settings
- Click on "Edit Profile"
- Then, navigate through to "Switch to Business Profile if otherwise, switch to Personal Account instead

Follow the instructions and enjoy.

One idea when using ads is to link your account with your Facebook using ads on its panel as well. Besides, create a short Instagram content story with its ads and get on engaging your audience. This is one of the most effective ways used by growing Instagrammers. Don't be left out, give it a shot.

Schedule your posts

At this point in your growth, you must learn how to be creative with the times you post. Go to previous chapters and revise the timing given on posting. In order to engage your audience, you have to get the arrangements of your post to suit every bit of your purpose. This is the aim of scheduling posts. The most important to consider is how your Instagram contents will have few gaps to keep the suspense of your audience.

- Shout out and show concerns to the top influencers

Many people feel special when they get good interest from people –so do top Instagram influencers. Try to make them feel more loved by getting consistently in touch with them. You can create a video talking to them and sending it as DM to them. If you are getting through from engagement group, the tab showing 'Following' will be at your disposal to sneak what these people are doing on Instagram. This is chiefly how this trick will get you more followers. You will be able to skim through the posts the people have an interest in, their comments and likes. You will be able to build your contents too around such and as well get enough followers from them.

Growing from your followers from 5000 to 10000

At this juncture, you will focus on building your followers with the steps you have learned. Try to create more creative stories to engage your audience. 10 thousand followers is a pretty large number to attain, repeat the steps given to you and you will be wowed with your success. Besides, consider monetizing your account. There are different ways of engaging your audience through your contents here. As a recommended example, you can use a tag that will enable other people to tag their fans as well, say #tag your mentor, etc. In the same vein, you could consider using a giveaway technique. For instance when someone tags or comments on a given post, they will be given a good price or anything.

Growing your followers from 10,000 to 20,000

Wow! This will look like mountain Kilimanjaro. You will wonder how on earth this is possible. At this point, try to abstain from any contents and posts not yielding the expected result. As expected, repeat the steps you have been using until you get the desired results. It could look like a trick to you, but it is attainable. Getting 10,000 followers and moving to 20,000 will open your account to enough opportunities. Make sure you grab every bit of them. Don't waste your time concentrating on the Instagram platform but rather build your social platform appearance and awareness. With this number of followers, you are more or less a problem solver and gift to the community. You have to design what people gain from liking and following your contents. There are various practical ideas for you to use in this stage; being a helper to answering the question on other websites such as Quora, detect forums within your niche and drop your contents there, create a blog site and write contents that will catch the attention of the viewers. This may seem very difficult to maintain at the first instance, but after consistent practice and experience, you will be used to it. You could reach out to people through shout outs as well. But before you use shout outs, grow your account to a considerable good number of followers as they can be expensive. Shoutout can be of a different type of Instagram like, photos, GIF and or video. When you are sorting for shoutout partners, you can talk to a friend to help you, but most of the time people charge for it. You must be careful because the aftermath of the shoutout is on good bio and post on your account. So, before resting on creating an expensive shoutout, build your account and make it catchy and audience-centered. Don't worry about how to get the number of people when they are not animals that are easy to get. Instagram has billion-driven active members; there are enough members for you. When you are contacted, try responding quickly in order to create a great impression. Make sure that interacting more with other top influencing Instagrammers is your aim —in comparison to posting contents. This is because with the good chain of people perusing your profile, even if you have only two posts, they will get the desired likes and comments which will build your profile to an amazing length. Every step provided from the beginning should be what you repeatedly apply at every stage of your growth. Also, applying the tricks from other previous chapters is recommended. In fact, go through them over once more after or during this chapter. No desired followers that can't be achieved once you have your right steps and enough resources to pursue such aim. At every stage of your growth, however, make sure you are doing enough fiscal analysis of the contents you have and how people are responding to them. As stated earlier, drop everything you are doing on growth that is not giving you what you want. Stay with these steps and watch your followers grow immensely.

Chapter 10: Secrets to engaging your audience when marketing on Instagram

While getting enough audience is a good indication of having a selling marketing platform on Instagram, engaging the audience is the key according to the Instagram algorithm. Recent 2019 reports on secrets to engaging your audience suggest that having followers of 5000 could prove profitable than just pilling 20000 followers without much engagement. A lot of followers become dummy without engagement and getting the best from followers as a marketing strategy lies solely on how engaging they are. Because of this disparity but crucial aspect of audience engagement, this section has been developed to take you through some clandestine ways of engaging your audience on Instagram. These are salient ways that create feedback-engagement with your audience. The tips given here are from the practical example of top Instagram influencers. Before going further, it is pertinent to give a short definition of audience engagement on Instagram. This is the process of getting your followers interactive. It is the process of receiving likes and comments on each of your post from your audience. To monitor the engagement of your audience, consider the following factors:

Comments

With these, you will be able to notice the feelings of your audience about your posts. They are a very impressive way to judge whether your followers are interactive/engaging. When you have good comments, there is a great sign people are expecting your contents. Of course, there are ranges of comments. Everyone can like a post, but when you are receiving enough comments different from such as 'Awesome' or 'Great' but something more creative, you have a great audience engagement. With good comments, your marketing platform is encouraging as you can easily track what people feel about your product and thus you will know the areas of likes and dislikes.

Followers

The number of your followers is a great yardstick to how people are engaging with your post. This type of yardstick is actually faulty as there is a different meaning to why people follow you. One can't solely rely on a number of followers as a shred of evidence in audience engagement for marketing. But followers influenced by your contents is a good indication of good audience engagement.

Likes

Actually, this is a good indication of people's acceptance of your contents. It is an obvious reason that could be rested upon as great audience engagement while marketing on Instagram. This is a good yardstick for you to judge.

Reposting and Shares

If you have a good number of followers ready to share your posts to their respective followers, it is a great indication of audience engagement on your contents. When your posts receive more reposts and shares, there is encouragement on how people have received your marketing strategy.

The above yardsticks given are all indication of audience engagement on your posts. They are things to look for when analyzing audience engagement and how to improve them. For a huge business with lots of followers, interacting with followers might pose some challenges. This is because there are lots of people to attend to manually. Therefore, there is a good necessity of knowing the secrets to engage with your audience while marketing on Instagram. You might not have gathered enough followers, but replying every comment might have posed challenges as well. So, below are some great secrets to increasing and engaging your audience while marketing on Instagram. The secrets are:

Taking advantage of Hashtag

A good hashtag guarantees an impressive engagement with your followers on Instagram. The importance of using hashtags can't be overemphasized. With the hashtag, you are sure your posts will get to the right audience and those solely within your niche. You use a hashtag to specify your posts on Instagram, and thus only those ready to engage with your contents are only receivers of the contents. The hashtag can as well be used to ask for the opinions, tagging of friends, asking your audience to take action, etc. on Instagram.

Posting creative contents

For a good turnout of your audience engagement, be creative with your posts. Don't just post like other social media platforms, make meaning out of each of your posts. Meaningful posts will surely give your followers the opportunity to interact with your posts. They will be triggered by the creativity therein. While doing your marketing on Instagram, try to be meaningful with your contents that people can relate with on Instagram. The photos you are posting must be designed to catch the attention of the audience. Likewise, let the contents that will be posted on Instagram be a typical reflection of your brand and product. With this in place, the engagement of you is assured as people now gain interest in your posts and your label.

Revolve your posts around audience interests

The number of posts you have should be controlled. Many audiences get bored with too many posts —even meaningful contents could be meaningless. But when your post is strategic, you create a kind of suspense in your followers which make them long for you. In fact, when they miss your post, they will search for you just to engage with the trend of the post. Posting just one video a day is enough for someone with a vision to increase the engagement of your audience on contents. The type of audience will surely influence when and how to post in order to get the best result of your posts. Make every moment count. In the previous sections, you have been taken through the process of getting the timing of your posting, check through them at this juncture for effectiveness.

Leverage on Instagram stories

This is an interesting part of engaging your audience with your stories. Telling stories on Instagram has proven to be one of the most effective ways to engage your audience in the marketing means. In early research on Instagram, people averagely spend like twenty-eight minutes using or viewing videos. Here lies your strength, create a short video of your products and post them for engagement. Make sure you are telling a story with each of your posts. They must be arranged in a chronological order to reflect the kind of story and brand you have. Many of your followers find it interesting to follow posts that are telling story brain-engaging stories. Don't waste this opportunity; leverage on the importance of this. It is marketing made easy; audience engagement is the true secret of marketing. Give your audience nice behind the scenes and practical usage of your product videos.

Using appropriate filter

Instagram has been designed with lots of filters to be added to your posts. They are not created for fun but rather to be used. It is all about getting the attention of any of your audience, so use the right filter for your post before posting them. That Instagram operates through visuals is a fact, if only you leverage on this while posting contents on Instagram. If you have captivating contents while marketing, your audience will be able to engage with your posts adequately through design. To get much of your audience's engagement, use a good filter that is appealing to eyes.

Use themes of Feeds

While lots of people know and use Instagram photo filters, many don't know nor use feed themes. This is what can create a kind of uniqueness in your posts. Because of little people's attention drawn to it, you have an opportunity there to use it as an instrument to engage your audience. Instagram visual is there to capture the attention of your audience. It is never a crime leveraging on it. With just a white and black feeds themes found on your account, many people will be lured to engage with your post. While many will be wondering how come you have white and black feeds, many want to know how and why you are doing it —remember it is to wow them all.

Create familiarity with Geotags

Very many people like to connect and engage with people around them, those they can reach. This is the work of geo-tags: showing your location or location of your brand and business. Make sure you add geographical location tags to your posts so that people around you could be aware of your posts. With good geo-tags, many of your followers will engage with each other. Some might even hang out outside Instagram. Lots of people relate to what they know, use this as an opportunity to spur more engagement of your audience.

Posting within the right timing

In the previous chapters, you have been taken through the times typical for a good audience. In addition to the times, the days are given as well. Posting in the right timing of your audience will increase the engagement of them to your content and post. When you have an audience of High school students, consider the times they are likely to come online and post on their feeds. Note that Instagram refreshes itself after some minutes in which the recent posts only are seen at the top of the feeds. You use social media publisher like Sprout to denote the times of your audience as well. Your engagement will be quick once your timing is correct.

Highlight stories on your profile

The feature of highlight, though transient, can be used to detain anyone that view your profile. The highlights have 24 hours life span, though they can be renewed. These features are great to entice lots of followers to your profile and chiefly engage them. They are a practical way to engage your audience on Instagram.

✓ Posts with CTAs on them

Wondering what CTAs are? Fewer worries, it means Call To Actions. This is a point where you solicit for the response of your followers. With a good CTA, many of your followers will engage with your contents. In fact, you can make your CTA a giveaway which will intensify the audience engagement. Perhaps you don't have any giveaway, asking the opinions and questions of your followers will also put them to actions. This most times creates immediate responses from your audience. It is really an effective way of engaging the audience on Instagram.

Creating contests

That people comment and reply to posts with incentives is a fact. Therefore, to get an optimum engagement of your audience, try to create tangible contests. Your giveaway might be a discount on your products, especially if it is a necessity for daily living. You could as well encourage your followers to tag their friends to benefit from this reward. The result or effect of actions such as this is drastic on your account as the post could even get out of the reach you have sent it. Anything can stand as giveaway contest provided the fight is worth fighting among the followers.

Establishing conversations with comments on your post

Replying to comments on your posts could as well boost the engagement of your audience in marketing on Instagram. One of the practical ways of getting audience interactions on your post is by establishing a kind of conversation. This conversation could be turned to chain talks whereby on a single talk, lots of replies from followers will spring up. If it gets too serious, you could be a hashtag creator and then your account is on the verge of reaching a good number of the populace –invariably your product and brand. With this continuous interaction, stable growth of audience is sure.

Engaging people with the same account

While following those top Instagram influencers, consider causing a huge conversation on their posts. With this, you could refer to your post with hashtags and their followers will check it out and then the conversation begins. Don't just follow them, create a kind of connection between your account and their account too. This is a great way to engage your audience, don't forget to include necessary hashtags.

✓ Measurement and Optimization of Campaigns

You will need to track the growth of your engagements at this point. This is to detect the areas with problems and strengths in your campaigns. Measure the engagement rate of your followers through the Instagram Engagement Calculator. With this, you will detect the behavior of your audience thereby creating a suitable post for them.

In conclusion, make sure you follow these steps but not by hook and line. Take those working for you and apply them for the best results. Repeating these steps is where the strength lies. While interacting at whatsoever stage, make sure there is no sense of spam or negative feelings. Even when people drop bad comments, reply with a colorful mood. With all these, many will consider your account as being responsible.

Chapter 11: Personal Branding

In a world of a million users, your technical and academic skills might do just a little or no good at all. So to be exceptional, you need to learn what personal branding is and improve your personal branding.

Knowing that you are a brand and marketing it so well to your advantage is what personal branding is all about. It is about emphasizing the very relevant aspect of you and how that is in line with what you do. It is not in any way about making a fuss of your personality but enhancing your intellectual, professional and personal characteristics.

David McNally and Karl Speak (1999) defined personal branding this way: "Your brand is a perception or emotion, maintained by somebody other than you, that describes the total experience of having a relationship with you."

Personal branding is the practice of people marketing themselves and their careers as brands. It was first introduced in a book titled "Think and grow rich" by Napoleon Hill and has been a necessity so far even till this age. Entrepreneurs, who want to stand out must do so by showing to the world why they are exceptional, and this is personal branding! There is always no second chance to make a great first impression. The more you work hard on branding yourself the right way, the more you are noticed especially by your prospective clients. Sell your own image through personal branding.

You might be wondering, how then do I market or brand myself? With access to the internet and social media, you can build an audience, position yourself as an expert, and start attracting clients for your business. That's exactly what a lot of people do. You must understand that personal branding is not a day's job and does not require just one action. It is progressive and involves a whole lot of work.

To define your essence, you just have understood yourself perfectly over time. Knowing who you are and what you are passionate about give you purpose and help you Brand yourself.

What makes up your personal brand?

Your personal brand is all about who you are, your essence and what problems you are a solution to in the market and world at large. It includes your resume, how you interact, how you look, how you speak, your values, etc.

It is exciting to know that your personal branding, though it represents who you are and what you stand for, it is ever evolving.

How to create your personal brand.

The basic thing that makes your personal brand distinctive from multitude is crafting your brand template. To have your personal brand, you need to organize every bit of your thoughts and creatively create a personal vision. As much as you cannot control every aspect of your life, creating a long term personal vision and working diligently towards achieving it will help you understand how your life will unfold. To create a clear and appealing image and reputation in the professional world, the knowledge of concrete things is needed. This includes;

1. Who you are

2. Where you want to be

3. Others who are worth emulating.

Who you are.

Understanding yourself better now will give you a hint to what you want to be in the nearest future. These following steps will give you a concise and better knowledge of yourself

1. Set your values. Your values are the core of your existence. They are what you look to when

making a decision. For examples, you might refer to your family, religion, intelligence, friends, etc. before taking important decisions in your life. These values define the things that are most important to you. The people, situations, etc. that make you happy the most is usually top on the list. Write them all out, without limit.

2. Prioritize your values. While setting your values, you would discover your values are not all equal. Prioritize your values by ordering them in descending order, listing your most valued as first. This is necessary in a case where you might be considering a new job that fits into your ambition but takes you away for long, from your home and family, negating your family and community values. Right alignment of your values makes you choose one over the other. Note that growing your brand personality is not just getting good sales but rather experience sportive moments with the profession itself. To be accustomed to your vision in personal branding, set laudable priorities on your values.

3. Discover your passion. Be careful not to mistake your values for your passions, though your passions and values may overlap, they are entirely different. Your passions are things that you spend your time on. For instance, your top value might be friends, but your passion is to spend the evenings at a table, discussing your discoveries and latest knowledge. Passion is what interests you and what you are ready to investigate even when you are not being paid.

Where you want to be.

Having known who you are, figuring where you want to will be less stressful and easy to figure out. Knowing where you want to be is for both personal and professional life. Here are a series of steps to guide you into knowing where you want to be.

1. Identify your strength and how they have been rewarding over time: Beyond your professional life, check the aspect of your personal life that

has been rewarding over time. Create an exhausting list of these aspects. For instance, while working at a retail shop, like customer service, you definitely do not like to encounter angry buyers, and this is a challenge. However, you enjoy listening to inquisitive customers, helping them with their questions and finding solutions to their problems. This is a strength, though you might not work as customer service in the future, you're a problem solver, and that is a strength that over time has been really rewarding for you despite all odds.

2. Group and align the strengths of potential personal visions: Having listed the strengths, group them into categories, narrowing them down to just five categories. This will point toward a list of professions that would meet your desire and give you fulfillment in your professional life.

3. Envisage the end of the career in the list: The previous step has helped you narrow down everything to a more specific list. The list of

professions now needs to be investigated. Imagine the end of the career and link it back to the initial stage.

4. Compare the career with your personal vision: Now that you have carefully traced your little beginning to this point, it is essential you compare by linking your discovered career with your initial values and personal vision before you get started. Locate the balance on your career where your satisfaction still meets success in line with your values and aspirations.

5. Embrace networking. As you grow your brand, it is vital to get connected to those of like passion. Grow your professional circle with peers, companies, and leaders around. The more your connection, the more relevant you are esteemed.

Chapter 12: How to monetize your account

After posting and spending on audience engaging contents, what comes out of it? There is a huge opportunity, a means of livelihood, lying at having good posts. Instagram launching of the Instagram plan has created lots of ways of generating money from posting. As one of the most influential social media platforms –has over 100 million and 300 million active users – Instagram was built on mere sharing of photos and videos, really. However, the innovation is given by Mark Zuckerberg, after purchasing it, created and widen the horizon of the platform. With the innovation, Instagram stands to have marketers, brand promoters and lots more. In this section, you will learn how to monetize those contents you have posted on your profile. It is pertinent to bear in mind that monetizing your account requires time –it doesn't come like magic. Every action around building profile for business relies on how to monetize the business account. While monetizing means using marketing strategies, it does not mean that your Instagram account will bring money like bot – this is not voodoo –it is a reality through hard work. Again, everyone might be right without going through these particular chapters based on their chosen activities on Instagram. In other words, if you have an account and you are engaging your audience, liking, following and posting great content, you might enjoy monetizing your account even without reading this chapter. However, doing every activity aimlessly will mar your account thereby disannulling you from monetizing your account. Therefore, here, as a matter of necessity, you will be taken through practical steps to monetizing your account on Instagram. These steps are:

Building strong followers

The chance of monetizing your account is proportion to having a good number of followers on social platforms. There are different means of getting followers discussed all over this book. To enjoy monetized account, you have to give growing of followers your utmost concern. In the algorithm of Instagram, one of the things that determine how early and grant for monetizing your account the number of followers. With a good engagement of followers using appropriate hashtags and Geo-tags, account monetizing will be done based on the number of visitors you have on your profile. Having good followers is the fundamental step to getting money from your posts on Instagram. As discussed earlier, the processes of getting followers include: conducting a contest, liking posts, etc. The process of monetizing your account requires you to do what your followers are doing to other accounts within your niche too.

The inclusion of links to your posts

Making money on Instagram requires you to put links to your sites at every post through the hashtags. Effective usage of hashtags to direct your followers to the products through link is very important. Endeavor to put link as hashtags to every photo of your products posted. With this, people will be able to look up the link and make a purchase. You have to note that clicking links is not yet enabled on Instagram. Therefore, your followers will have to copy the link to their browsers in order to visit it. You can as well include the link in your bio and redirect them through the hashtags.

Posting photos of high quality

Instagram has always been used for social marketing. This is because it operates through posting and sharing of visual: photo, video, and graphics. To monetize your account, you need to post high-quality pictures. With high-quality images, many more followers will be enticed and, thus, will follow you. Consider posting current pictures of your products. Make sure the right message is passed across using the appropriate grids. Quality photos make it easier to locate your products and increase your sale (monetize the photo). You can do well to post photos of real-life situations of your products as they give courage on their potency. This is another way to monetize your account.

Get creative with Instagram Video feature

Most times, in the growth of follower using contents, photos might not convey a million ideas in your brain —you just wish to add more. Don't be depressed; there is a feature on Instagram that is 15 seconds long video. This video is there for you to increase your creativity with contents on Instagram. Meanwhile, you don't have to get the video clumsy -a reason for giving your short seconds- keep it simple. Make sure you find a way of including the link to which the products can be purchased while uploading the story videos. Create a problem and provide the solution through your product. This will give you a better chance of having enough follower and invariably, monetized account.

Involve your Followers

In the monetization process, getting your followers involved in the process requires you to ask them post photos on their experience with your products. You don't have to post the pictures of your products alone, try to post contents on your followers and fans. Tell them to take a picture of where they are using the product, then, compile everything into a video, for onward posting on your feed. As the video goes viral with necessary hashtags, your followers and their fans will get the feed thereby promoting your brand. The more pronounce your brand is, the better the chance of getting money from your account —monetizing your account. To encourage your followers, you could include incentives, like discount on the purchase of the products, etc. for the person with the highest post impression. This will not only promote your brand but also keep people's gaze on your account for subsequent opportunities. It is a great way to make money with your Instagram account.

Conducting Contests

The importance of running contests on Instagram recurs at every benefit of having an account on the platform. The reason is that people are inspired by what they get than giving. To monetize your account using contests, you must do everything for people to follow and like your posts. Create a very good campaign with nice giveaways. Try to hasten your followers by putting a deadline for your contest. Make sure you tell them to tag their friend upon liking the photo. With this, you will make money by pushing many people to do a contest that will get you what you want. Imagine getting 10,000 followers to do your contest and just only one person will be chosen, this is great. After the contest, make sure you post the photos of the winner with hashtags for validation of your contest. No sooner had you done this than lots of followers will rush into your account taking you PR back to the first trick of monetizing your account discussed.

Solicit for Client Testimonial

There is nothing more convincing than seeing practical evidence. Client testimonials are Visuals from your followers. These are photos relating to how effective your products are through your followers. When these Visuals are submitted you, make sure you hashtag the user and the link to the product itself. Everybody seeing this will surely not only follow you but also buy from you. This is a great way to monetize your account really.

Use Influencers or celebrities

To get your products across to a large audience, use celebrities or top Instagram influencers. Many of Instagram influencers share the pictures of the brand they are using, and by this, the seller of the brand gets more sales. Make sure you put noticeable details on the brand so that people will contact you effortlessly. You can search for Instagrammers with a very high number of followers, send them DM and get your brand promoted and monetized.

Using specific Instagram tools

There is nothing to be done on Instagram that does not have tools used. It might not be effective though. There are lots of tools used to monetize account on Instagram, and they have proven effective over time. Some of these tools are:

Posts
On the schedule of times and days of posting on Instagram, this tool is the way out. Posting

contents are an effective way of marketing on Instagram. Getting the engagement of your followers is the key which lies solely on the days and times they are online. This tool, through your setting, will post your contents to fit your targeted audience.

Repost
This works in a unique way. When using this tool, it reposts other user's posts and gives appropriate credit to them where it is necessary. Using this tool will open your account to lots of opportunities as top Instagram Influencers' posts are connected to your account. Amazingly, the location of your brand is added to the repost.

Piquora
When sourcing for selling contents to post, this tool will generate relevant contents that will match your niche. The visuals collected via this tool are unique and selling. You don't need to panic on the approval of your contents since the

ones generated are collation of most sourced contents.

Iconosquare

This tool will help you To do the statistical analysis of your profile, Getting the number of followers, likes, and comments on your posts are what you enjoy with this tool. With this, you will be able to calculate the impressions people get on every of your post so that you can adjust in the subsequent ones.

Chapter 13: The best methods for selling products to customers as a small business or personal brand

The ability to sell through specific strategies is the compelling idea for a small business owner or personal branding. Convincing people to buy your product especially novel product or small scale business might be arduous. Sometimes the sales dwindle one time more sales, the other less. A good business maintains some percentage of sales within a given period of time. The best and effective method to make sales as a small business firm depends solely on the type of business. You have to be strategic in the way you handle your sales. Never be too concerned with how to make a profit –though it is the primary aim. There are no best methods anywhere though, but these strategies will, in one way or the other, affect the level of your customers. There is no one way to getting customers, study your own product and do the needful. Top product sellers use specific strategies; these are combined and put together. Here, you will learn practical methods for selling your products to customers as a personal brand. The best of these methods are given below:

Understand your product

The fundamental strategy applicable to any type of personal brand or small business is a perfect understanding of their products. You can't afford to conceive questions from your customers without giving appropriate answers. Every growth in sales boils down to your ability to convince customers. If you don't understand your product, giving convincing evidence to why someone should buy your product above others will be difficult. You have to be used to your product, know everything about your brand and you are on your way to great sales. This will require always to see the possibility of your products solving real-life situation problems.

Act and don't show

Many people believe and use products with effectual practical evidences. Showing people your product, as many have traditionally believed, will add little or nothing to sale rate of your product. Rather, the ability to give practical essentiality of the product will do the sales lots of good. You can get testimonies of your buyers and use it as evidence. Be careful not to bore people with lots of talks as even the times you don't have sales in mind; many will run away or avoid you. Instead of talks, act by showing them how effective the product had been. To show people practical evidence is equivalent to saying that the product has fulfilled why it was invented. With this, many customers will never think you are money monger rather someone who cares about their wellbeing. You are assured good sales as a personal brand or small business, with this strategy. Give the customers the chance to examine the product because they feel safe with their own experience –no one sees the truth and believes lies.

Know your customers

With a good knowledge of who your customers are, you have a perfect understanding of their needs and wants. Because you have known their needs, you will tailor your sales along with them for sales increment. Many customers might even think you have known them, someone, to have described their wants in perfect terms; everything lies in your ability to understand your potential customers. This is an effective way to make sales, even if your product is an invention. The demography of your customers should be a prime factor you will consider as well. Solicit for a recommendation from other Customers

After you have got a few customers, you could make more sales with them. Try to tell them to be your referral. This will increase your sales and invariably profit. Try getting them involved in suggesting your brands to people. You might need to include incentives in order to encourage them to do more. With a good referral, you are assured an increase in profit as the process of making is done by more than one persons. You can even keep St this strategy throughout your branding processes: more you get customers the more you increase referral and then sales. You will grow a community of buyers with this strategy, keep at it.

Consider your customers in pricing your product

In the process of pricing your products, you must consider your primary customers. When the price of your product is not proportional to your customers, it is either you have low sales or people have a feeling of unsafe. If you have your low sales, it means your price is too high, and if it is negative feelings, your price is too low. You have to consider factors such as this in pricing your products.

Give customers an adequate audience

Whenever you are with customers, make sure you give them rapt attention. Let them ask questions or talk while you answer them accordingly. By no means will you engage in an argument with your customers. Make them feel like a boss. Pay attention to every detail of what they want and how they want it done. Give them every advantage they deserve: Deliver their goods on time, constantly relate with them. Listen adequately to their suggestions on your product, most likely, it is the way people perceive your product.

Create a great relationship

For anyone that wants a big sale, knowing your customers is of great importance. Let them feel you care about them. You have to build a long term relationship with them. You could visit them in their domicile if need be. Keep to their likes and dislikes. Ask for their health, be a friend to them. Everyone loves to be loved, show your customers, genuine love; they love to do anything for you. With a great relationship, you are sure of your customers' financial status –they wouldn't buy all the time, but love must be shown all the time.

Keep in touch

Always keep in touch with your customers. You could contact them often to know the state of their health and how they are faring. Get their mails and send them messages frequently on how you would love them to be your permanent customers. Always communicate the new trends you have, so as to gain much of their interests.

Use the customer relation scheme

A customer relation officer is someone that cares for clients on behalf of a company. When you use this scheme, you are guaranteed that even people you cannot communicate with are intimated on your products. They are professionals who have been trained in the way to relate with customers to bring about an increase in sales, so you will need to have them. Though you are running a small business or personal brand, customer relation is another phase of the business entirely. Overall, consider your profit and how buoyant you are before considering a customer relation officer.

Request for your sales always

The aim of doing anything outside the primary reason for having a business –making profit through sales –must be maintained. Whenever you call or have an encounter with the customer, make sure you remind them of how you would love them to make a purchase. Again, you have to be strategic, don't make them feel that was the reason for your visit or call in the first place –a healthy relationship must be maintained. Don't be too ashamed to mention your product;

everything lies in how you approach the customer.

Chapter 15: How to incorporate a unique selling proposition into your personal branding

Personal branding, as the name implies, requires you to do your branding yourself. Everything within your capacity is to your advantage in personal branding. For example, influence around your family and friends prior before having a brand will help your personal promotion of your brand. There are limitless opportunities lying ahead of you if you have many things innately built even before having your brand and business. The unique selling proposition is an attribute of service, business or even person that makes it distinctive. This is that unique touch you have on your brand and business that distinguishes it from every other closely related product. That there is no new thing under the earth is a fact. Then, how do you create that special touch to your brand? Unique selling proposition is that feature why people should buy your own product against others. It is used to define the position of your brand in the market place. Amazingly, being unique is equivalent to your personal prowess. Combine your strength and incorporate them into your brand and you will stand out. This unique selling proposition will make you have edged ahead of every competitor –even if they have their market ground already. The deal in creating a unique proposition is to sit down and strategically outline the strength that made you human. You cannot separate your personality from business though, so take you're into play in your business.

Knowing personal branding and unique selling proposition, you may ask: how do I incorporate a unique selling proposition to my personal branding? Before answering this question, you have to take note of the fact that every question on unique selling proposition boil down to the kind of brand you have. There are brands that do not need any special or unique touch in them but rather in their packaging. Everything that makes a distinctive personal branding is every process from the production to the final consumption of the brand. If you have services, your own branding might be so different —don't worry you learn them here. Now back to the question of incorporating unique selling proposition, the processes are very simple. The ones treated here are gathered from the top influencers. They are:

Identification of your Unique Selling Proposition

As a unique selling proposition is a way to a distinctive brand, its identification is the inception of its incorporation to business. You have to know your unique proposition before you can use in to sell or promote your branding personally. Just as the saying that a problem known is a problem solved, so is the identification of a unique selling proposition. When potential customers encounter your brand amidst all other competing ones, the probability of them selecting your brand is premise on how

pronounced your unique proposition is to them –
this is why the unique proposition must be
glaring. To identify your Unique selling
proposition, you have to define your customers.
Don't get your targeted customers clumsy; have a
clue of who they are. Having known them, you
will be able to get their likes and dislikes which
will promote your brand among other
competitors. Make sure you make a thorough
research on your close competitors. This is not to
copy them but rather to know their areas of
weaknesses, and they build yours around them.
This will help you in your personal branding: it is
a great means of incorporating your unique
selling proposition to it.

Make sure your brand outstandingly appeal to potential customers

After the identification of your unique selling
proposition through your potential customers,
appealing only to them is the next key in the
incorporation of your unique selling proposition

to personal branding. There is no sole way to appealing to your customers; however, there are practical things included in your branding. To specify your customers, you will have to include boldly those people that the brand is best for. For example, you are branding a belt product used for people with big Tommy, include such statement as "girdle belt for ladies without flat Tommy." With this, you have done lots of things such as specifying the gender, the purpose of the belt, etc. This means that guys with big Tommy can't use it, pregnant ladies or a lady with big Tommy as a result of the accident and so on, will or should not buy it. In fact with good specification, retailers of your product will know where, when and how to sell your product. They will provide a guide to using it when necessary. As much as you have the intention to narrow down your product consumers, don't, by any means, underestimate the strength of your brand. Specify your customers and maintain your product when you are incorporating a unique selling proposition to your branding. The basic idea here is that when you narrow down your target to the specific customers that you want, the uniqueness of selling proposition to your brand is guaranteed.

Take advantage of your unique nature into the Industry

You have to build a good social perception of your brand. This is to say use the advantage of how unique your products are to build a good reputation for it. You can't afford to recruit workers with bad social reputations as this will distort the trust and courage to buy from you. Don't be surprised to know that a certain group of people use or buy a product based on the person that they have seen using it. With a good reputation, you can be sure that many and everyone around you know who you are and how that selling a fake commodity will ruin the trust built for you. This is to say you must build a personality of honesty and trust. In your branding, make sure you give the duration of the result or influence of your product should you be branding health-related products. Let everything be plain, and you will see that your uniqueness will tell how your brand and sell your products. This building of a strong trust is a uniqueness that you could leverage on in your personal branding, after all; personal branding could be read as personality branding.

Avoid a competitive mind

It is about time you stopped thinking about other products brands and focused on yours alone. Many business developers always have a competitive mind, especially in personal branding. They would want to know how to outshine their competitors. While being aware of competitors could be helpful in improve on your product, it could mar it too. Instead of being concerned about the brand around, why not try to create things that will be different. You have, at least, being in the community for some times, create something that can barely be found elsewhere. You could use the judgment of people to do your feasibility study. That is, you could create a questionnaire on the product or on the weakness of the existing ones. Be less concern about competitors in branding your products personally. Try to develop something unique yet indispensable in society. With this, even if you have a high price, many will be 'forced' to buy from you. Develop a mind of the invention and try to create a needful brand. If you have this uniqueness developed, your personal branding will be mounting a great sale within few times.

Be known for your business

Very many times people who brand their products personal forget the fact that they are part of the product. To ensure a unique selling proposition, try to grow with your business. Using celebrities is not a bad idea. The point is that you must be part of the business, get into it. You have to use or be a personality that suits the branding yourself. Create lots of connections between how you look or are perceived and your brand. Everything you are doing is to ensure a healthy branding platform. You have to be careful, however, in your choice of celebrity or models. For example, if you are selling clothing and you chose a celebrity or better still, model, you have to keep using the model throughout your brand. Besides, you have to select the model based on the fact that there is a huge correlation between the person and your product. It could sound funny to know that when someone known for your brand takes up another brand, there could be a drastic reduction in sales. Be consistent with the person. For consistency sake, you have to be extremely careful in your selection –carelessness might not be an excuse.

There are lots of unique selling propositions that could be incorporated into your personal branding. The main thing to do is to establish a good proposition based on yourself and the brand. The lists given here might not be enough –it might not even be applicable to you –try to consider your brand before creating a good proposition to your branding. Devise your own proposition, act on them and increase your sale. But with good hope, these steps should be applicable to you, no matter what.

Chapter 16: How to Access opportunities that can take your brand to the next level

There are different opportunities that can be used to promote your brand. It is assumed at this stage that you already created your brand and that you are using Instagram as a marketing vendor. After all this, it is pertinent for you to know how you could promote your brand to the next level. By promotion, it means how you could give your brand that professional touch that will attract that dream you have for creating it. Having a brand is different from promoting it. Many people with great ideas and brand loss their brand because they could not take it to the next level. This wouldn't affect you because you must have implemented some, if not all, of the tricks and secrets, are given from the inception of this book. In this section, you will be given some tricks on how you can take your brand to the next level. No matter the level of your brand, it will always require your effort to move it forward – sometimes maintain its stand. There are two basic ways to accessing opportunities to take your brand to the next level: passive or active. Passive access is the one got by using some 'indirect' tricks chiefly without your direct involvement while the active access requires the direct input of accessing the opportunities. The process of accessing opportunities, here, are combined (not separated as passive or active). They are:

Establishing a good network

This involves you meeting great professionals within the niche of your brand. This will open you to lots of opportunities like knowing your competitors, learn different strategies to your business, getting recommendations, and so on. You will have to relate with them in a way that you will be opened to opportunities. Many might not show you the direct access, but with your inquisitiveness, you will learn a great deal from them. There are different strategies that you can use to establish a network of brand promoters. These are:

- Joining their group: you have to be part of these groups and keep yourself updated with their meetings in order to promote your brand. There are lots of these groups online, the source for them and join them.

- Requesting answers to sensitive questions: You have to participate in the group. Ask questions in order to engage other people too on the platform. You will learn a greatly from fellow brand promoters.

- Give the introduction of your business when necessary: You have a great opportunity here. Tell them the uniqueness of your brand and the incentives that you offer. Make sure you tell them that you are open to business partnership.

- Give out your cards: Select people that have an interest in your brand and establish communication with them privately. Give out your cards at the appropriate time. Know more about them and take your time to intimate them more on your business. Let them the opportunities that lie in your brand partnership.

Conducting Advertisement

To gain access to opportunities for your brand promotion, you must do much of your business advertisement. Advertise your business to create more awareness. There are different ways of how advertisement could get you opportunities which are:

- Placing your advertisement in newspapers, journals, magazine and all: With a good advertisement in selling and popular newspapers, you have a better opportunity to promote your brand. Newspapers, journals, etc.

could go a long way even to the most remote part of a state, so advertising there implies your brand goes the way of it too.

- Going commercial: This means that you take your brand to television or radio station for promotion. This might be expensive, but it is a great way to promote your brand.

- Sending mail: You can promote the brand by sending mails to your potential customers. You can include merchandise or coupons in the mail, just make it engaging and interesting.

- Using the internet SEO: When you open a site for your brand, ensure that the content on it is SE optimized so that people from anywhere might be able to locate it. With good SEO contents on your brand, you are sure that when people used a search engine, your brand will be one of the top-rated options.

- Using billboards: To get opportunities on your brand promotion, create billboards on it and place it in a strategic place where lots of people can see it clearly.

- Using experts: To enhance your work, you could use experts that will do publicizing your brand. They are trained for it, so they know the special means to go through it.

Establishing a good relationship with renowned organizations

Try to create a good relationship with organizations that have a name already. Do some collaborations with them to ensure your promotion. However, many organization might not want to collaborate while those who would require some payment. You could be lucky though to meet a good one. Use the advantage of the organizations so that you could build a good ground for your brand.

Use social media platforms

Having learned marketing through Instagram in this book, you are sure of the power of social platforms. Rest on the power of the social platform and create lots of opportunities for your brand. Use the appropriate campaigns and hashtags to promote your brand. Knowing that social platforms have lots of members therein, using them for promotion will tell greatly on the brand as it will open it to lots of benefits. With a good usage of the social platforms, you are assured of the great opportunities your brand have.

Make use of free gifts

By gifting out, incentives upon purchase of your goods could encourage sales and open your brand to opportunities. Try to incorporate gifting to every purchase of your brand so that many customers would be enticed to your brand. With incentives, many customers will inform many of their friends and family to benefit from them. By this, your brand is opened to opportunities to access.

Establish healthy relationships with clients

As expected, a good relationship will promote every brand. When people don't like your brand in the first place, having a good relationship with them could strengthen their love and increase sales. Try to make your customers loved; they are humans too; they are not banks. Remove the feelings of whether you only need their money, though mentioning your brand at every opportunity given is encouraged. Build good personal connections between you and your customers all the time. Look after them any time you notice they are drawing back, perhaps they are sick you could know.

Use real-life testimonials

The effect of using your clients to do an advertisement for brand promotion can't be overemphasized. Many people believe and trust what their fellow said than what you say about your product. You will need to implore your customers to do some sort of advertisement and encourage to tell people about the effectiveness of your brand. This will give your product a quick recognition, and many will want to try out the brand thereby creating more opportunities for its promotion.

To be open to opportunities, you need to be prepared for the opportunities themselves. This is because when there are accesses to benefits for your brand growth, and you can't hold them, they will slip off your hand. Therefore, it is recommended that you put all things in place to catch every opportunity around. There are no specific times to when these opportunities, they will come at random; preparations too should be around this.

Mark Hollister

Chapter 17: How to use business storytelling to sell products in both physical and online market places

Over the years, a whole lot of things have changed but so little have changed about humans and the human mind, and this includes the fact that we have the same core emotions, we like talking about people we know and like, or find useful, and we still have the same way of storing information. So to !make people remember you and your business often and tell others about it you need to appeal to the mind and this is effectively done through catchy, fascinating and efficient brand storytelling.

When talking about branding strategies, brand stories have become one of the hottest tools in building brands in the world today. A brand story becomes effective when it appeals to the audience's emotions, sticking a particular picture in their minds. The brand stories inspire, motivate and attach the audience to the brand. To start with, you must understand, fully, your brand, its attributes, persona, etc., and once this is done you are just a few steps away from creating a compelling story for your brand, to sell your products both online and in the physical market place.

As a first step, know the progressive life cycle of your brand so far. Know the start, fall, decline, an offshoot. To develop your story, you must understand how your brand started, those who bought it and why they did, a decline (if any) in sales, etc. Notice the change over time. This is a good start to develop your story. Be acquainted with every detail, no matter how small and insignificant it might be.

Furthermore, take note of and precisely write down the attributes of your products as seen by your audience. For example, your brand and product might be seen as useful, durable for a lifetime, motivating, etc. This is essentially important to be included in your narrative. As much as possible, avoid being false about your description, be sincere and avoid untruthful attributes of your brand. In continuation, no story is a story until characters are introduced which are compelling and identifiable. After which you create a plot. This plot has to be specific and directed towards a specific type of tried and tested plot. Be reminded to Keep the brand story succinct and impressive.

In order to sell your products using business storytelling, employ this formula PSM. The PSM formula (acronym) represents Points, Story, and Metaphor.

1. Point. Your point should be blatantly stated. It should be a one-sentence point with an aggregate of the whole theme. For example, in advertising a product that relaxes the muscle of the body, the point could be "Stress is the problem but relaxation and comfort can solve it." This is the supposed theme of the entire story, compressed into a line of the word referred to as Point.

2. Story: At this segment, you talk exhaustively on the point and how much that it has both negative and positive aspect of the already stated topic. An exposition of the point is what is done here, how the product came to be, what it has done and how it's been thriving over the years is what interests people than you think. To every brand, there is a story, tell yours with integrity and purpose.

3. Metaphor: The metaphor reiterates the point but in a dynamic way. Explaining the story from a different angle. Integrating the point and story into synchrony.

Note that the above-stated formula is your rough draft of what your story would be and not the story nor the narrative. Having dealt with the basics, painting a nice picture of the brand in a story will no longer be difficult.

Goals in creating a successful brand story are

In the eyes of your ideal audience, you are presenting yourself and brand as

1. Motivating and inspiring to them

2. Educative

3. Challenging and/or

4. Emotional.

The power of brand storytelling

As humans, stories are the center of our communication and how we share or relate information. More often than not, our usage of stories to pass information is higher than a few talks we have. Is it therefore as impactful in business, branding, and sales? Of course!

According to research stories have been discovered to be more memorable 22 times than just facts and figures. Therefore, when used strategically, storytelling can enhance the output and sales of your brand and product.

It is scientific proven too that our neural activity increases when being told a story. It sparks up our emotion and lights up the sensory cortex of the brain making you feel, smell, taste and even imagine the story being told. And since a diagrammatic representation has been processed in the brain, it sticks in there for so long than other facts and information just plainly stated. It has been said too that it enhances neural coupling in the listener and he/she tends to relate the story his/her experience, thoughts, and life.

Incredible, right? You can light up your customer's brain and appeal to their emotions by creating an emotional story too. A well-told story will not only appeal to your audience but will keep you outstanding among the crowd.

Why is brand storytelling important?

In competitive market places, brand storytelling gives people the chance to connect. Believe it, people work, consistently, with you, your brand and product when they believe in what you do, and they feel a connection. These connections are essential and lead to engagements because the client and audience see themselves as an integral part of the brand and deems it fit to work with you. These engagements get people activated. They seek opportunities to help you tell your story to others as well.

Tips for implementing your brand story

One thing is to create a brand story, but an essential part is to implement it. Every thought and interaction counts and must bring your brand to life your brand story should clearly and obviously communicate your message and what you stand for in a sentence.

1. Be consistent

An inconsistent story and message make your efforts less impactful. Every representation of your brand (logo, store, etc.) should be consistent and without dilution. So as to resonate your intent to your audience. It is important to note that you do use totally diverging branding styles for products of your single brand. Your products should complement each other and fight for attention.

2. Have an authentic brand story

Having poorly crafted branding or a lack of authenticity is due to a lack of knowledge about what you do and why. This is why it is important to lay background information about your brand. Knowing intently the in and out of your brand.

Knowing that the audience and potential customers are smart and they can sniff out every iota of insincerity, it is important that your brand story authentically represent your brand and products exceptionally.

3. Document your brand story.

With credibility, authenticity, and consistency being a distinguishing feature of your brand story, it is necessary to document them as this will help you to be more successful. Documenting your brand story will help you keep your story intact away from being misunderstood or misinterpreted. It will keep your employees, audience and potential customers on the same page as you since it serves as a guideline. The necessary information to document includes but is not restricted to the following

- The start, pea, and end of your brand story
- Your mission, vision and !mission
- Your slogan
- Your logo, visual designs, etc.

Examples of great brands:

1. Coca-Cola

Though Coca-Cola is tagged to sell carbonated sugar and water by a few. But they have always been about happiness, fun, joy, and friendship. And they have been consistent towards it as seen in their logos, designs, advertisements, and campaigns.

2. DevaCurl

DevaCurl's product on haircare is especially for women with curly hair and how to care for it.

This has been what their entire brand story has been about. DevaCurl understands its core target audience and works towards it so well.

Conclusively, brand storytelling reinforces the bond needed in marketing. It gives your brand the voice it needs to communicate as though it was from human to human. Your story should be formal, catchy and consistent in its theme. Know that storytelling is beyond what you say but how you say and communicate your message and how it connects to their audience. Your audience and customers define your brand, study and understand them, their needs and hold these facts so dear to your heart. Learn to choose your words wisely too. It is expedient to know that brand storytelling is not a boring, blog post nor a long, five-paragraph essay about your company. It is not a tool to manipulate your prospective customers and audience.

Bonus Chapter: Instagram Automated Tools

Having discussed by and large on Instagram marketing in 2019 using practical steps from top Instagram influencers in order to guide you through the hurdle of social marketing. For everyone using Instagram as a means of social marketing, this book is the way out for a successful growing your personal brand. Automation of account is very important because of the nature of the platform –consisting of a large number of people. Because of this, the aim of everyone using Instagram as a marketing tool will fully harness with the automation. However, the reason for creating a chapter on using automated tools after much criticism on it as they won't serve the ideal purpose of the business brand is that growth of personal brand will equally require them. When you have grown your business to a level, it will be hard somehow to be doing many works manually. This is because liking and following of lots of people and post to like 20,000 or more will surely require automation. As cautioned throughout this book, don't grow followers with bots as when you will need them for engagement and all, you will lack as if you never had them ion the first place. The tools here have been arranged and selected to suit personal brand growth. You have no problems using them as proper consideration, and examination has been given to them. Whether you are a beginner or you need more followers, these tools will be of help. As a beginner, you will use it for your quick growth while for intermediates, you will use it to ease the arduous work. That there are lots of works done as a business marketer on Instagram makes it a necessity to be aware of tools as an escape route. Employ these tools where it is necessary. You have to know that most of the tools require little money before using them —you will need to buy them. Also, you will be taken through what is used to build the tools and how they are built.

The tools are those validated in early 2019 because many of the archaic ones used are no more use of the stage Instagram has grown to. These tools are:

- **MEGA follow**

This makes you noticeable on Instagram by every user within your niche, though. In the automation process, you would need to keep your clients on a long term base. While you could forget them, you could even get messages from them without replying, Mega follow will keep your track on each of your clients. As stated earlier on paying for using tools, Mega follow is sold for $8.99 only. The result of this tool on your account, to say, your brand at large worth paying even more as more customers equal more profits.

- **The Social captain**

This is one of the tools that grow followers automatically and as such when you are using a business account, engaging your followers to yield brand promotion will be difficult. However, for someone that use other means that rely solely on the number of followers, the social captain is the true way to this. When you activate it on your account, you grow followers automatically, and you stand a chance to enjoy benefits attached to having that number of followers. This is great, really. You will receive engagement from this tool as it will arrange itself accordingly. It won't be perfect really, but at least before your responses, something will fill in. Likewise, you can set the tool within a few time and input special things like words you want to receive. This tool has a variety of set up suitable for whatever purpose you want –through its primary function is to get followers automatically.

- **The Falcon Social**

To increase your followers, you will need some special training especially if you are a beginner. While social captain grows followers automatically, falcon social tool increases it – they work hand-in-hand. Apart from growing your followers, this tool provides a step-by-step way of doing it. This means that those whose aim is not to use the app but to learn the process of growing followers will also find this tool interesting. This tool works 24/7; whether you are online or not. You can set up long term plans on how you want it to operate, and it will work accordingly. You could as well, with this tool, set a way to respond to comments which could be either mail or DM on Instagram. This means that any contents on your account would be siphoned such a way that the link in their bio will be contacted automatically.

- **The Social upgrade**

On the menace of using bots to creating followers, the social upgrade has been the tool devised to cure it. When using this app, your account will be redirected to an account manager who will take care of every activity on it. You will only do less work by providing answers to questions when necessary. The growth of your account it sure as this tool will generate every important information for your growth and their managers.

- **The Instajool**

Following people manually on Instagram becomes a herculean task for a business account with lots of followers. On the basis that maintaining a healthy relationship on Instagram require mutual activities from both followers and those following, you always need to follow people. This tool is an accelerator to your account. It will increase and follow instantly while you are receiving likes and comment from users outside your community. Amazingly, Instajool is not a special software or app: it is an optimized feature contained in every browser. All you need is to search for it and link it to your account with simple steps. Apart from being an optimized tool, Instajool is easier to access and use for varieties of functions. Automating it is more easy and efficient with your account, whatever the need you have.

- **The Instabow**

On the note of posting contents on your feed, Instabow can be used to post contents from any links. Apart from posting, this tool use necessary captions and hashtags so that your posts will get to the targeted audience. It works in a fantastic way as it is regarded as one of the best Instagram automation tools. Remember we discuss timing and days for posting contents? Instabow is that special tool that can be used to schedule your contents based on your targeted audience. To say, this tool work just like humans will do. There is no difference in what you enjoy on contents that Instabow will not work out in a more convenient and accurate way. In the process of creating stories with your posts, Instabow will help you post them and do that in chronological order or sequence of the stories' plot. If you are running more than one account and you would love to posting on them consistently at different times, this tool will enable you to post contents among more than one login. With this tool, you can vacillate through different accounts at the same time with different contents. Among these accounts, Instabow recognizes the chronological arrangement in the stories as well. This is a great tool, obviously.

- **The Instafluuu**

This tool is also known as a secretive online bot. This tool work in such a way it will give your account that online appearance it deserves even among any influencers. You will operate this tool with just three simple steps: recognition of your competitors, providing their details of your account and submission.

Step I: Recognition of competitors: This tool is actually used to appear online among any top leading user. With this, you will need to get the details of those top influencers whose posts are always seen among many people. You input their details on the tool and move to the next step.

Step II: Supplication of personal details: After you have input your competitors' details, you will need to supply your own your details so that Instafluuu will be able to trace these account with yours and do the necessary. Of course, the competitors must be people within your niche. The next thing is to click a simple in-built button on the page you are.

Step III: Submission: You wouldn't need to supply any details anymore, rather submission so that your data will be processed and give you the desired output. This is the point at which the tool works like magic. Your contents will not only outshine those leading influencers, but it will also retain a stronger feed section even when the news feed refreshed itself automatically.

With Instafluuu, your appearance online will grow faster, and many people within your niche will be aware of your brand. Many of them will, however, take you as a strong rival, therefore prepare your contents and account to answer every of their expectation. Many opportunities will be opened to your account as top leading Instagram users will be willing to partner with your business not knowing you are only a starter. This is really great, and many people have been sourcing for tools such as this. It is a spy and trick that takes your account and invariably, brand to the next level and create increment in sales.

- **The Instamber**

On the fact of generating real people on Instagram, Instamber will serve you right. It serves lots of purposes in the process of generating followers. Its functions include liking, following, commenting, etc. throughout the Instagram platform. There are different phases in this tool however, which are: the tool that controls and put together the comments you have on all your post, a tool that takes care of the following and likes, the tool that could be used for DM for any type of messages to your followers, and the tool that is used to arrange and schedule your contents to suit the timing of your audience. As part of the tool that is activated with money, the Instamber goes for $10 monthly.

- ### The Following Likes

When you have different types of software linked to your account, it might be very difficult to control them. This is the work of Following Likes tool. It controls all the other apps and maintains their functions on all of them. Interestingly, Following Likes works for any social platform which means that you can add it to any of them at the same time. It moves each of your activities forward. It is very vast in function on any social platform.

- ### The InstaVast tool

Every social marketing strategy should involve using this tool. Every marketer will surely need InstaVast tool in order to hasten the process. There are different types of phases on this tool which will be work effectively for everything you wish to do during marketing. It is also referred to as the most effective marketing completing tool.

For everyone doing marketing, it is easier for you; this is an aid for you. Though some of the features there are paid for most of all are not free. To enjoy the fullness of this tool, combine it with your own marketing manual strategies taught throughout this book.

These tools might seem expensive, but their function is much more significant than what they cost. They will help with any kind of activities you wish to do. In order to enjoy the totality of Instagram marketing considers putting all or some of these apps on your account.

It is important to know that the way these automated tools are built determines their functionality. Therefore in the following part of this chapter, you will be learning some general features of the tools. The one chose here, i.e., Marstagram is the basis of automation.

Instagram Automated Tool: Marstagram.com

Instagram is a great platform filled with all kinds of people from all walks of life. With one running a business account on Instagram, it is pertinent to keep an eye on the followers' profile in order to promote one's business. Not only business profile but also personal profiles as there are many chances of winning lots of goodies for having a fast growing profile −this is expected from any platform as a way of compensating clients. However, it is important to have or gain courage in one's profile and as well keep track of everything that happens through and on one's profile.

Instagram automated tools have different functions such as: following anyone that follows you, automatic likes, automatic comment on any hashtag you were mentioned, etc. Everything handled for the better understanding of your Instagram profile is done by the marstagram automated tool. The fast-growing of your business is guaranteed. This is because Instagram is one of the vast platforms where online marketing for business takes place. There are lots of advantages attached to using an automated machine. Obviously, human power cannot be equivalent to the machine. Your business has come to experience much reformation and growth. Do you have much followers and you feel it is impossible to attend to them? Never panic, Marstagram works effectively.

Benefits of using this Instagram automated tool include but not only the following:

- Fast and safe

Sequel to the nature of Instagram, generally, comprising of lots of people, it is almost impossible to keep track of activities manually. This automated tool helps you to perform functions without asking on individual feeds. The actions are taken accurately without much ado. It saves time and energy. There is no manual input required, just subscribe to Marstagram and experience an automatic response on individual accounts of your followers.

- Automatic tracking of followers' account

When you have followers, you will be able to follow them automatically. You must not be online all day long. Every prescription you gave is closely followed. As well, you will be able to comment automatically on any post or hashtags you have.

- Adoption of more followers

With Marstagram automated tools, people will be able to search for your account effortlessly. The potential customers, peradventure you run a business account, will be able to follow you and be followed automatically.

- Automatic engagement of users

In cases where you are not online, and you have some things going on your profile, this automated tool will engage the followers accurately without the person knowing. This is most effective for people with much followers which requires more attention that only machines could offer.

- 24/7 working hours

This automated tool works over the night. If you have followers from around the globe which their time is different from yours, this automated machine works even in the night. There is no rest or pause. Effective working of your profile is assured. There is no need to even, at some time, attend to activities anymore with this tool.

Instagram is a fast growing platform undisputedly. The creation of Marstagram takes about 45 days without delay. The Marstagram site which is pure automation of your Instagram was created through MGP25 Instagram API and PHP language. The PHP language is basically used for the database which is used to store information of both followers and the followed.

Concerning the usage of MGP25 Instagram API is basically for feeds on Instagram. It integrates the hashtag content on the website pertaining to the feeds from the followers. You can print your photos from the feeds on your Instagram profile. The API can be used to count the number of likes on a particular picture which could be used to create a rage.